THE PROSTITUTE IN THE FAMILY TREE

THE PROSTITUTE
IN THE FAMILY TREE

Discovering Humor and Irony in the Bible

DOUGLAS ADAMS

Westminster John Knox Press
Louisville, Kentucky

Book design by Jennifer K. Cox
Cover design by Alec Bartsch
Cover photograph © Elena and Walter Borowski, 1995.
A late nineteenth-century family, circa 1880, courtesy PNI.

First edition
Published by Westminster John Knox Press
Louisville, Kentucky

This book is printed on acid-free paper that meets the
American National Standards Institute Z39.48 standard. ∞

PRINTED IN THE UNITED STATES OF AMERICA
98 99 00 01 02 03 04 05 06 — 10 9 8 7 6 5 4 3 2

Library of Congress Cataloging-in-Publication Data

Adams, Douglas E.
   The prostitute in the family tree : discovering humor and irony in the Bible
   / Douglas Adams. — 1st ed.
        p.   cm.
   Includes bibliographical references and index.
   ISBN 0–664–25693–7 (alk. paper)
   1. Wit and humor in the Bible.   2. Wit and humor—Religious
aspects—Christianity.   3. Storytelling—Religious aspects—
Christianity.   I. Title.
BS680.W63A33   1997
220.6—dc21   97-16943

For good friends with good humor and profound creativity:

Curt Anderson, Dan Apra, Bob Bradbury, Margie Brown,
Glenn Bucher, Dennis Campbell, Joan Carter, Carla De Sola,
Steve De Staebler, Jane Daggett Dillenberger, John Dillenberger,
Gordon Dragt, Jim Duke, Allen Dyers, Ted Estess, Don Fado,
Durwood Foster, Clarice Friedline, Bob Funk, Mary Ellen Gaylord,
Steve Hanning, Bill Herzog, Harland Hogue, Conrad Hyers, Bill Jacobs,
Mary Jacobs, Cindi Beth Johnson, Eliza Linley, Charles McCoy,
Thor Mickelson, Margaret Miles, Jo Milgrom, Michael Morris, O.P.,
Michael Moynahan, S.J., Bill Nelson,
Tim Nuveen, Jane Owen, Jennie Winsor Payne,
John Rogers, Wayne Rood, Clark Sterling, David Steward,
Margaret Taylor, Jack von Rohr, Ray Welles, Cynthia Winton-Henry,
and Tom Woodward.

CONTENTS

1

The Prostitute in the Family Tree

The Telling Humor of Biblical Stories
as Grandparent Stories

Remember the stories your parents told you about what it was like when they were growing up and how hard they worked? Now remember the stories your grandparents told you about what your parents *really* did when they were growing up. Both parents and grandparents tell stories, but the content varies: Parents tend to clean up their stories; grandparents tell stories that are more truthful and have many rough edges. Parental stories are solemn and can kill by prescribing an ideal we cannot fulfill, but grandparent stories are humorous and give hope and life by sharing a reality similar to our own.

Biblical stories are like grandparent stories. Jesus, Paul, and the Hebrew scriptures tell stories that include rough edges—unethical or ambiguous characters, unresolved or surprising endings—and so we laugh and know that we and others may live through the rough times in our lives, too. Biblical stories present patriarchs, matriarchs, and disciples not as perfectly faithful and ethical persons whom we could not hope to emulate but, rather, as persons who are often immoral, unfaithful, and thickheaded. Therefore, in spite of our own failings, we, too, can hope to be disciples. Persons who think the early church was perfect are often in despair concerning the state of the contemporary church and no longer attend when ministers and people quarrel. In the light of Paul's descriptions of the divisiveness in the early churches, however, even our present churches look good.

In our culture, we do not hear enough grandparent stories. Many parents move their children far away from their grandparents, and many grandparents have retired to Florida or Arizona. Some grandparents do not act like grandparents, while others are in nursing homes where they are not often heard. I tell the following anecdote so we can have an understanding of grandparent stories before we explore the biblical ones.

In the second grade, he played baseball with the Pee Wee League before he grew up to play Little League ball. His next-door neighbor was the coach. This little boy was fascinated by a stopwatch the coach carried to time plays; and he saw a lot of that stopwatch, because during weekend games he was usually next to the coach on the bench. After practice sessions during the week, the coach and his wife often invited the team into their home to eat ice cream and watch the first television in the neighborhood.

On one of these occasions, the coach and his wife were called away and asked the little boy to lock up the house when the others had gone. After finishing off the ice cream and turning off the television, he noticed the stopwatch on the dining room table, so he went over, picked it up, and began pushing the buttons. The dials went around and around. Then it was time to leave, so he put the stopwatch in his pocket and went home.

As noted in *The Confessions of Saint Augustine,*[1] Augustine had the wisdom to steal pears he could enjoy in private. The trouble with stealing a stopwatch is that it is a social instrument: One needs to time someone else. The little boy kept the watch in his pocket all week long until the baseball game on Saturday; then, in the midst of a big play, he pulled it out of his pocket to time the action. Sitting right next to the coach, he was exposed as a thief.

That night, the father called the boy in for a talk with him and his own father. He began by saying, "Son, you have ruined your life!" (The boy was only in the second grade, but parents give you the impression that once you fail your life is at an end.) He went on to say, "You might be forgiven once; but if you ever steal again, you will be branded a thief for life. Then you will never be the doctor or lawyer I hoped you would be." (The father didn't realize the boy could still be a minister or a teacher.) He turned to the grandfather and said, "You tell him how serious this is."

The grandfather leaned back and said, "It *is* pretty serious. Of course, it could have been worse, like the time your father stole the Johnsons' boat up at the lake. It took me two days to get him out of jail. Or there was the time your father and his friends were graduating from high school and rented a cottage on the edge of town; they all got drunk, wrecked the place, and landed in jail again. And the third time your father was in jail—"

The father interrupted, saying, "I think we have talked enough about this."

Grandparents give you the impression that you can do it wrong once, you can do it wrong twice, and you can do it wrong three times—and there is still hope. There are no "three strikes and you're out," either in grandparent stories or in biblical stories. How many times does Peter deny Jesus? After he denies Jesus three times is Peter out? No; he becomes the head of the church.

Humor gives us hope. Heredity and environment are not the absolute arbiters of what will be, as Jesus' genealogy details in the first chapter of Matthew's Gospel. As Gardner Taylor, an African-American preacher in Brooklyn, noted, Rahab the prostitute is in the family tree of Jesus Christ. This is really something to wrap your mind around.[2]

Many years ago, I created an annotated genealogy of Jesus to remind us who those characters were so we might see the humor and how it undercuts determinism. For example, a fine king, Jotham, was the father of a very bad king, Ahaz; but Ahaz was father to Hezekiah, who restored the kingdom to justice and piety. Hezekiah was the father of Manasseh, who ruled fifty-five years and was evil for all of them. The good news is that, if out of the worst can come the best, there is hope for our children.

There is already one annotation in the genealogy, an annotation in verse 6, which shows that it is a grandparent story. It says, "David was the father of Solomon by the wife of Uriah." A parent would have noted that David had slain Goliath or united the kingdoms or written some of the psalms, but the Gospel reminds us of David's sin: lusting after Bathsheba, making her pregnant, and then setting up her husband to be killed by the enemy.

I accompany the annotations with cue cards (noted in brackets) so that a congregation or class will know how to respond even if they miss the annotations. There is a card labeled CHEERS for the likes of Jotham, BOOS for Ahaz, APPLAUSE for Hezekiah, HISSES for Manasseh, and HUH? for about a third of the remaining characters, about whom we know nothing except their names, since they are not mentioned anywhere else in scripture or history. There is some humor in having a long string of such unknowns before Joseph, Mary, and Jesus. If out of complete nonentities can come the Messiah, there still may be hope for presidential administrations. With some characters in the genealogy, their ambiguity requires cheers and boos to express their characters or our responses.

An account of the genealogy of Jesus the Messiah [CHEERS, AP-PLAUSE], the son of David [CHEERS], the son of Abraham [AP-PLAUSE], who pretended Sarah was his sister, let Pharaoh have her, and received many cattle [BOOS].

Abraham was the father of Isaac, whose name means laughter [CHEERS]; and Isaac was the father of Jacob, who stole his brother's birthright [HISSES]; and Jacob the father of Joseph and his brothers, who sold Joseph into slavery [BOOS]; and Judah the father of Perez and Zerah [HUH?] by Tamar, who played the prostitute [BOOS] for the sake of justice [CHEERS]. Perez was the father of Hezron [HUH?]; and Hezron the father of Aram [HUH?]; and Aram the father of Aminadab [HUH?], and Aminadab the father of Nahshon, a fine captain of Israel [CHEERS]. Nahshon was the father of Salmon [HUH?], and Salmon the father of Boaz by Rahab, the prostitute [BOOS] who saved God's people [CHEERS]. Boaz was the father of Obed by Ruth [CHEERS], the faithful foreigner. Obed was the father of Jesse, the father of King David [CHEERS].

And David was the father of Solomon [APPLAUSE] by the wife of Uriah, whom David had set up to be killed [BOOS]. Solomon was the father of Rehoboam, who was faithful to God through much of his reign [CHEERS] but abandoned God for five years [BOOS]; and Rehoboam was father of Abijah, who had fourteen wives [CHEERS, BOOS]. Abijah was the father of Asaph, who abandoned God at the end of his life and died of gangrene of the feet [HISSES]; and Asaph was the father of Jehoshaphat, and Jehoshaphat the father of Joram, and Joram the father of Uzziah, whose pride brought his fall [BOOS]. Uzziah was the father of Jotham, a very good king in every way [CHEERS]; and Jotham the father of Ahaz, a very bad king in every way [BOOS]; and Ahaz the father of Hezekiah, who restored the kingdom to piety and justice [CHEERS, APPLAUSE]. Hezekiah was father of Manasseh, who ruled as king for fifty-five years [CHEERS] but was evil for all fifty-five years [HISSES]. And Manasseh was father of Amos, and Amos the father of Josiah, and Josiah the father of Jechoniah and his brothers, who were all faithful to God throughout their lives [CHEERS] and were all deported to Babylon [HUH?].

And after the deportation to Babylon, Jechoniah was father of Salathiel [HUH?]; and Salathiel the father of Zerubbabel, a wise governor chosen by God [CHEERS]; and Zerubbabel the father of Abiud [HUH?], and Abiud the father of Eliakim [HUH?], and Eliakim the father of Azor [HUH?], and Azor the father of Zadok [HUH?], and Zadok the father of Achim [HUH?], and Achim the father of Eliud [HUH?], and Eliud the father of Eleazar [HUH?], and Eleazar the father of Matthan [HUH?], and Matthan the father of Jacob [HUH?], and Jacob was the father of Joseph [CHEERS], the husband of Mary [APPLAUSE], of whom Jesus was born who is called the Messiah [CHEERS, APPLAUSE].[3]

We experience the humor when we see the whole story, but we miss the humor when a text is taken out of context. A grandparent story can become a parental story if only a part of it is told, to moralize, as often happens in teaching and preaching. For example, in chapters 2 through 5 of this book, we will see the humor in Jesus' parables and miracles when we look at all the details in each of those stories and understand them in the context of the first century. If one glosses over the details and the context, one misses the humor. Similarly, in chapter 6, we will see the humor in Paul's letters when we look at the whole chapter or the whole letter—a humor missed if we take a verse out of context. In chapter 7, we will see the humor in Hebrew scriptures when we remember the whole story of each person rather than only one episode.

For example, there is no humor if we take the end of the book of Jonah out of context and forget the beginning of the book. At the end, Jonah turns self-righteous (an occupational hazard) and urges God to destroy the Ninevites because they had earlier disobeyed God's laws, even though they finally repented. Jonah insists that, as an object lesson to others, God must destroy those who disobey him. In a play by Jim Groves and Terry Teigen, God responds, "If I were to wipe out everyone who disobeyed me, I wouldn't have anyone left to talk to. We certainly wouldn't be carrying on *this* conversation."[4]

God's response reminds us of Jonah's own early disobedience, a disobedience his later harsh self-righteousness tries to cover up. Whenever we see such harsh self-righteousness (as in the parable of the unmerciful slave detailed in chapter 4), it usually reveals an attempt to cover up the person's own failings. Professor James A. Sanders at Claremont School of Theology believes that biblical stories are mirrors for identity and not models for morality.[5] That is another way of saying that biblical stories are grandparent stories, not parental stories. If we clean up the biblical stories, we can no longer identify with them; if we share the full story, we can see ourselves in them.

By reading the whole story, we see the rough edges and the humor. In worship and education, the arts allow us to present the whole story and so help people see the humor. Each chapter in this book shares not only insights into the biblical context but also methods to present the whole story and its humor. For instance, when in chapter 7 we do a Phil Donahue-like interview of Abraham and his families (Abraham in the middle, Sarah on one side, and Hagar on the other), everything Abraham says sounds funny. If one were talking just with Abraham, he might tell only of his faithfulness in leaving his homeland or in being willing to sacrifice Isaac; but when we see him in the company of Sarah and Hagar, we remember the whole story, including his immoral actions in Egypt and elsewhere. That most preachings and most teachings about Abraham have selectively told only those episodes of his faithfulness demonstrates how parental and moralizing we have been as preachers and teachers. It is no wonder that many persons know little about humor in the Bible, because we have shared so few of these biblical stories from the pulpit and in our study groups.

By missing the humor in a biblical text taken out of context, we do more than miss the laughter; for by viewing a verse of scripture as solemn when it is meant to be humorous, we often get the opposite message than that intended. An example is the well-known verse (usually taken out of context) where Jesus says, "Give therefore to the emperor the things that are the emperor's, and to God the things that are God's" (Matt. 22:21). That verse was actually a punchline for a joke on some of the Pharisees who were later revealed in their impiety. But by taking it out of context, it has been viewed as an eternal statement of principle separating church and state, with results quite the opposite of what Jesus intended. Before World War II, Cardinal Innitzer quoted the verse out of context when he urged the people of Austria to "Render unto Hitler the things that are Hitler's; and render unto God the things that are God's" and to welcome Hitler into Austria. I have heard a southern judge use those words of Jesus to chastise Martin Luther King, Jr.'s mixing of religion and politics.

We see the humor in Jesus' words when we look at the whole story (Matt. 22:15-22). The passage begins by noting that some

Pharisees took counsel on how to trap Jesus in his discourse and sent some of their disciples along with some Herodians to Jesus. As real Pharisees are the most ethical of persons, there is already something questionable about any Pharisee who would conspire with Herodians; for Herodians were the party of Herod, who would bend the Jewish law to get along with Rome. Real Pharisees disdained talking to Herodians, much less plotting with them.

I usually ask a congregation or class how many of them have quarters in their pockets or purses, and I pick out some with quarters to be the Pharisees and others around them to be Herodians. Then I note that these Pharisees may be phony Pharisees, for real Pharisees were not likely to be with Herodians. I ask everyone to look for the trap in the question the Pharisees pose to Jesus: "Is it lawful to pay taxes to the emperor, or not?" (v. 17). What will happen if Jesus answers, "Yes, pay your taxes"? He will lose his popular following, for people do not want to pay any tax, especially one that forces them to acknowledge that Caesar is their lord. But we know that his answer does not mean "pay your taxes," for at the end of the story he has not lost his popular following. What if he should answer, "No; do not pay the tax"? Then he would be jailed by the Romans for urging people to break the law. As he is not jailed at the end of the story, he did not say no.

As usual, Jesus does not give an answer to a question but instead poses another question. He says, "Why are you putting me to the test, you hypocrites?" (v. 18). Their hypocrisy will be revealed in the rest of the story. Jesus adds, "Show me the coin used for the tax" (v. 19). When they produce the coin, they reveal much about themselves. Jesus emphasizes that revelation by asking "Whose head is this, and whose title?" (v. 20). Before all the people, the Pharisees and the Herodians proclaim the name: "The emperor's" (v. 21). (To bring out this awkward moment, I sometimes have Jesus, in a dramatic rendering of the text, ask them to repeat that answer a little louder for all to hear. In saying "the emperor's" and in carrying such a coin, they reveal much about themselves and their loyalties.)

Notice that Jesus calls attention to both the head and the title. Such coins showed Caesar presented as a god, with the inscription CAESAR, KING AND SON OF GOD. Having shared that information with my congregation or class, I then turn to the Pharisees and Herodians and say, "So you are carrying around a coin in your pocket that breaks two commandments at once." Rome minted other nondescript coins to avoid this crisis of conscience, and truly faithful Jews were not likely to carry coins with Caesar's image. These Pharisees and Herodians are thus exposed to ridicule and revealed as Caesar's creatures. So there is a satirical edge in Jesus' closing words, "Give therefore to the emperor the things that are the emperor's" (v. 21), for it is evident that these Herodians and Pharisees are "the things that are the emperor's." When I say these words, I look them up and down and emphasize the word "things." Then I pocket the coin, as I say, "and to God the things that are God's" (v. 21). Robert Funk suggests the humor in that last phrase by noting that there is no indication that Jesus ever returns the coin. Funk sees Jesus pocketing the coin, which the Pharisees would be unlikely to ask Jesus to return.[6] That same day (Matt. 22:23–33), the Sadducees try to trap Jesus with a question about the resurrection. He eludes them too; in Luke 20:40 it says that after that encounter "They no longer dared to ask him another question."

I do not give back the quarter to the person who provided it but, instead, keep it, explaining that if I gave it back the story would be forgotten. By my keeping it, that person will always remember this story; and I will double my honorarium. This story does not tell us whether we should pay our taxes or not: that is, it is not a parental story providing a model for morality. Instead, it is a grandparent story or a mirror by which we can identify ourselves, revealing the commitments of those in the story and allowing us to reflect on our own commitments.

Because the humor can be missed easily in a reading of that passage, I urge use of mime or drama when presenting this scripture in worship. Jesus points to the Pharisees and Herodians with the words "things that are the emperor's" and pockets the coin with the words "things that are God's." The nature of the original trap laid by the Pharisees and Herodians is made evident by the mimes or actors, who pose the question slowly. On the words "Is it lawful to pay taxes to the emperor?" the common people in the crowd take a step or two backward, shaking their heads negatively. Then there is a brief pause; and on the words "or not" a Roman soldier leans forward very close to Jesus and awaits suspiciously the potentially treasonous answer. A giant coin (as large as two feet in diameter) may be created with Caesar's image adorned as a god and a clearly visible inscription proclaiming him KING AND SON OF GOD. This would then be handed to Jesus by a hesitant and embarrassed Pharisee, who produces it from inside his robe when Jesus asks for a coin. Or a large drawing of the coin may appear in the background when a normal-sized coin is handed by the Pharisee to Jesus. The latter method has the advantage of allowing Jesus to pocket the coin easily at the end of the scripture reading.

Another example of how the larger context helps us see the humor in Jesus' words is the saying of Jesus, "If anyone wants to sue you and take your coat, give your cloak as well" (Matt. 5:40). From studies of first-century social context, we know that most people wore only two garments: the coat was the outer garment, and the cloak was the underwear. A person could aspire to perfection by giving his or her coat to another person who asked for it; but that person should bring the coat back by nightfall or the giver could be very cold. We can imagine the person who wants to earn his way into heaven coming to Jesus and raising the question: Must one really give one's coat if anyone asks for it? Jesus' response undercuts such a quest to earn one's way into heaven as he says, in effect, "If anyone wants to sue you and take your outer clothing, give him your underwear as well." The questioner, not wanting to be naked, might draw his coat more closely around himself and say, "I don't care to be saved that much."

John Donne caught the humor in those words of Jesus. Donne is known to us as a poet, but he was also a preacher to lawyers in training at Lincoln's Inn. In one sermon, Donne said to them that Christians "will not depart from the literal understanding of those words of our Saviour, 'If any man will sue thee at law for thy coat, let him have thy cloak too; for if thine adversary have it not, thine advocate will.'"[7]

Fractured Families and Busted Banquets

The Wounded-Healing Humor of Jesus' Parables

If Jesus' parables were parental stories, they would concern such things as a perfect family, a perfect dinner party, a just manager, a just judge, a merciful slave, and a rich wise man; but his parables are grandparent stories, about a prodigal family, a busted banquet, an unjust manager, an unjust judge, an unmerciful slave, and a rich fool. If Jesus had told stories about perfect families and perfect dinner parties, we would despair at the families we have and never dare to entertain at dinner; but in the humor of his parables, we are able to find hope in our own imperfect families and invite others over to eat with us.

A close reading of the text in Luke 15:11–32 reveals the rough edges of each character. The Bible does not call this story "the prodigal son," although a moralizing parent would call it that, and many of us as moralizing preachers have called it that too. When we look more closely at the text, we see prodigal qualities in both the elder son and the father, as well as in the younger son. Thank God this story is not about two sons who always got along well and a father who always acted wisely and succeeded in reconciling them; for such a perfect story would make it impossible to live with the brothers and fathers and sons we have.

As the story opens, we see the rough edge of the younger son, who says, "Father, give me the share of the property that will belong to me" (v. 12). What would your father have said to you if you said that to him? When I have asked people that question, they have variously responded that their fathers would have said (expletives deleted), "What property?" or "Forget it!" or "Get out of here!" Normally, property comes to sons only when the father has died. So the request insultingly treats the father as dead and is like saying "You are dead to me, old man; give me my share of property in your will." Even the father of a juvenile delinquent might at least ask, "What do you want it for?"; but the father in this parable "divided his property between them" (v. 12) without comment. What property does that leave the father? None: an important fact to remember for what happens later.

The story then notes that soon "the younger son gathered all he had and traveled to a distant country, and there he squandered his property in dissolute living" (v. 13). At that point, I turn to some fellow in the congregation or class and say, "What is dissolute living? You look like you would know." That person usually responds, "Wine, women, and song." The Greek term, *asotus,* may mean either sexual immorality or simply spendthrift living or excessive, uncareful living such as failing to keep the checkbook balanced or investing in the stock of Pan American just before it goes belly up. Many people tend to interpret "dissolute living" as immoral living, because at the end of the story the elder son, who is angry with the father for killing the elder son's fatted calf for the younger son, asserts that the younger son "has devoured your property with prostitutes" (v. 30). We might ask, "How does he know?" He lies twice immediately before saying that, so we may doubt what he says. I ask the group how many of them *have* elder brothers and how many of them *are* elder brothers. They laugh and know that elder brothers often try to put younger brothers in the worst possible light, no matter what the truth.

Even after the first few lines of the parable, we know quite a lot about the elder son precisely because he has not yet appeared. He apparently took his portion of the property without protest, while he might instead have said, "Father, you keep the property, for you are still head of the household as long as you live; and may you live for decades more." As the elder son in a Jewish family, he should be responsible for reconciliation, but he twice fails in that responsibility early in the story, first by not reprimanding the younger son when he treats the father so disrespectfully and later by allowing the younger son to leave. To gather all that he had would have taken the younger son quite some time, during which the older son could have acted but did not.

In the distant country, the younger son "hired himself out to one of the citizens of that country, who sent him to his fields to feed the pigs" (v. 15), hardly a kosher occupation. When "he came to himself" (v. 17), we should not read that as repentance; such a phrase merely means a lightbulb went on and he got an idea, which could be good or bad. Notice how self-serving the idea is. Instead of thinking, How I have hurt my father; I will go back and see what I can do to make him feel better, he thinks instead, "How many of my father's hired hands have bread enough and to spare, but here I am dying of hunger!" (v. 17). This is not thoughtful repentance from the mind or love of father from the heart but a little lower: the thought of getting food for the stomach.

Then he devises an equally self-serving speech to say to his father. Most of us have devised such speeches to get back on the best possible terms with parents, lovers, or friends when we have offended them. In the third grade, I ran away from home but got no farther than the back steps. I sat there for what seemed like hours but was probably only ten minutes, trying to come up with a speech to reconcile with my mother without having to do the dishes for a month (a few days, maybe, but not a month). Remembering what he thought when he came to himself, we see how devious this speech is. Its climax is "Treat me like one of your hired hands" (v. 19), which means, Give me bread; for when he came to himself, he remembered that the hired hands had bread enough to spare. The beginning of the speech may be calculating too. Having treated his father as dead, he now addresses him as "Father." He might calculate that such a term will win the old man over; but notice that he does not deliver the whole speech he devised, which was to have been "Father, I have sinned against heaven and before you; I am no longer worthy to be called your son; treat me like one of your hired hands" (vv. 18–19). He never delivers that last request.

We would expect the son to go and prostrate himself before the father, who would remain seated in the Near Eastern fashion; but as the son was still far off, "his father saw him and was filled with compassion; he ran and put his arms around him and kissed him" (v. 20). At this point in the telling, I rush toward a man in the front pews, embrace him, and lavish kisses on the top of his head. Laughter results from this surprising turn of events.

What should the son say now? His speech, designed to get him back into the good graces of the father, is superfluous. The father has taken him back. He should say "Thank you," but this kid never says thank you. He prepared this speech and by heaven he is going to give it, whether it is appropriate or not. Have you ever written a letter which became inappropriate because of a change in circumstances? Yet, having invested time creating such a fine letter, you are tempted to send it.

The son begins with the speech he prepared; but notice that he never gives the last part. As I read out the speech, I pause as I hear the father saying to bring out the "best" robe, "a ring," "sandals," and "the fatted calf" (v. 22). My next line as the son should be "treat me like one of your hired hands"; but in repeating that line to myself, I say, "The hell with that," rip up the speech, and then say "Bring on the party, baby" and rush to embrace a woman and join the crowd.

We never see the younger son again. If he were truly repentant, might he not seek out the older son, who is not at the party? If he were really repentant, might he not stay close to the father and notice him leave the party to talk with the older son in the courtyard? All we know during the rest of the story is that the younger son is at the party.

Having taught worship, preaching, and the arts for over twenty years at Pacific School of Religion and the Graduate Theological Union, I receive each year many sermons and worship services from former students. I notice the problem when looking at the worship services, even before reading the sermons: They often include only verses 11–24 as the gospel reading and ignore the last part of the story in the sermons as well. When I write back and ask what happened to the rest of the story, they respond, "My people like happy endings, and that last part is so acrimonious." I write back and say, "Do you slash paintings also?"

In the last part of the story, the older son comes home and hears the music and dancing. Music and dancing accompany or follow dinner, so we may assume either he has been left out of the dinner or he chose not to come. The next line in the story makes it clear he was not even invited, for he asks what all this music and dancing means. If he had been invited but simply chose not to come, he would at least know what was going on. That the younger son did not invite him, we can fully understand, given the younger son's selfish nature; but apparently the father was so excited about the return of the younger son that he forgot the elder. So the father is not perfect either.

Asked to explain the music and dancing, the servant is wise enough to respond with a minimalist message, for messengers can get killed for the message. The servant responds, "Your brother has come, and your father has killed the fatted calf, because he has got him back safe and sound" (v. 27). Notice that the servant does not mention the best robe or the ring or the sandals. Whose fatted calf is that and whose ring and robe? All of them belong to the older son, for the father divided his property between them. Well might the servant not mention the ring; as some scholars note, this could be the signet ring that conveys control of all the rest of the property.

Understandably, the older son "became angry and refused to go in" (v. 28). He knows what he should do—the older son should be head of hospitality—but no one even bothered to invite him to eat his own fatted calf. The father comes out and pleads with him to go in to the party; but he refuses with a response that contains at least two lies. First he says, "Listen! For all these years, I have been working like a slave for you, and I have never disobeyed your command" (v. 29). Having just refused his father's plea to go to the party, it is a lie to say he has never disobeyed a parental command. Second, he says, "Yet you have never given me even a young goat so that I might celebrate with my friends" (v. 29). As the father gave him half the property, including this fatted calf, it is also a lie to say the father never gave him even a goat. It is the older son's own business if he never chose to use the calf to give a party for his friends. In the face of those two lies, we need not believe the older son's final assertion that the younger son "has devoured your property with prostitutes" (v. 30).

The story ends with the father and older son arguing outside. As with most parables of Jesus, there is no ending. As James Breech has detailed, when there is no ending, there is no final judgment.[1] Any of these characters may yet change. Endings normally include what happened to each person: The good person went to heaven and the bad one to hell, for instance. In contrast, Jesus' parables are cliff-hangers like the episodes of a soap opera. Will John return to Mary? Will Bill get the promotion? We do not know. Without endings, there are many possibilities.

With congregations or classes, I ask people to imagine and share several possible endings, for Jesus honors the intelligence and activates the imagination of the hearers when he does not supply one for us. People have suggested many endings. In one, the father returns to the party and the older son lingers outside; late at night, after most guests are gone, the younger son drunkenly walks outside, where the older son reaches out from the shadows and strikes him dead. That ending fits many other biblical stories of brothers, like Cain and Abel or Joseph and his brothers. In another ending, the older son finally relents and goes to the party with the father, but then, in greeting the younger son, he sees the family ring on his finger and in a rage cuts off the younger son's hand and has the father committed as senile for giving away property not his own. In a third ending, the younger son goes off with the ring, best robe, and other property and, after losing it all, comes home again.

He repeats the pattern again and again and is still periodically living at home at age fifty. In still another ending, the older son goes in to the party, and he and the younger son are finally reconciled; but in another ending, the two sons continue to live at home unreconciled. In a sixth ending, the father gets sick of both sons, takes what is left of the property, and goes off to Las Vegas.

Why did Jesus tell a grandparent story of such an imperfect family? Why not tell a parental story of a perfect family where brothers love each other and the father never bungles? Parental stories can kill you, as I learned when I went off to college. My parents had told me that our family had always done well in college, and I should do the same. Why do parents lie or tell the truth so selectively? It is a well-intentioned attempt to encourage us to do well. My impression was that they had gotten As in all subjects, and the first year I did very well.

The problem arose at the end of my sophomore year; I neglected second-year French when thoroughly immersed in a research paper in history, which I loved. In the final French examination, I wrote down all the answers I knew in fifteen minutes; it was a two-hour exam. I prayed to God, who either does not know French or was not telling; and then I knew I was going to fail. I had never even gotten a *B* before. I felt ashamed and could not call my parents. Thoughts of suicide went through my head; *that* is how the perfect parental story can kill you. Not daring to call my parents, I phoned my grandmother instead. I blurted out, "It's the end of the world." She responded, "What's wrong, Dougie?" It is hard to take yourself with full seriousness when someone calls you Dougie; that is why we lock some grandparents away, for they are the only remaining persons who call us by our baby names. I persisted in making a penultimate thing into an ultimate and said, "It is all over for me at school. I failed French." Grandmother started laughing; she laughed and laughed. When she stopped laughing, she said, "Oh, just like your parents. They never could pass languages either." My parents had never told me that. Thank God she did, for it saved my life.

Before introducing Jesus' parable of the great banquet, I ask people, What is wrong with a perfect dinner party? They respond that a perfect dinner party is boring or that it kills sociability; for if others give a perfect dinner party, we can never have them over to our house because we cannot reciprocate. I had a perfect couple in one congregation I served as pastor. When they arrived at church, they would sometimes rearrange the altar flowers that had been arranged by others; the worst part of it was that everyone had to admit the flowers always looked better after they had rearranged them. People hated that couple because they were perfect. I could like them because I had their kids in a youth group, and they made it clear their parents were not perfect. The kids let me see their mother's studio, which was a mess, as is true for many artists: half-finished canvases, spilled and spattered paint, and dirty rags scattered on the floor. I thought that if the other church members could see that studio, they might begin to like her. Well that would be expecting a lot; but at least they might dislike her less.

That messy studio was on my mind when I agreed with the couple's offer to hold dinner parties at their home after Sunday worship so old members and prospective members could meet. It was disastrous to the church sense of fellowship, for the dinner parties were perfect. The children served without question. The house was immaculate (we never got into the locked studio). The soufflés rose perfectly. The wines were just the right temperatures. The conversation was scintillating. After dinner, the children offered to clean up without being asked to do so. Now everyone hated not only the couple but their children as well. People complained, "How can we ever have them over to our house with the children we've got?"

Thank God, Jesus did not tell the story of a perfect dinner party. In Luke 14:15–24, one of those who ate with him clearly thought it would be perfect when he said, "Blessed is the one who will eat bread in the kingdom of God!" (v. 15). But Jesus said to him, "Someone gave a great dinner and invited many" (v. 16). In the parable of the great banquet, everything goes wrong. People who have been invited, and have accepted the invitation, fail to come when the slave goes to tell them everything is ready.

Their excuses for not coming are all questionable. The first said, "I have bought a piece of land, and I must go out and see it; please accept my regrets" (v. 18). Would he not have looked at the property before buying it; and what would he see of it out there at night? A second person said, "I have bought five yoke of oxen, and I am going to try them out; please accept my regrets" (v. 19). Would he not have tried them out before buying them; and how would he try them out at night? But at least both of them were polite and extended their regrets. The third said, "I have just been married, and therefore I cannot come" (v. 20). At first that seems a reasonable excuse. If he has just gotten married, he has better things to do! Yet, when one thinks about it, why did he accept the invitation a week or two before if he knew he was getting married? Ah, maybe he did not know he was going to have to get married. In any case, this man does not even extend his regrets. James A. Sanders details that these three excuses were appropriate ones for Jews to be excused from going to war, as noted in Deuteronomy 20:5–7; for the authorities did not want people going into battle whose minds were on property not yet put to use or marriages not yet consummated.[2] But in this parable, the characters inappropriately give excuses for not going to war when it is a celebration, not a war, to which they are being summoned.

When the slave reports these excuses to the master, the master is understandably angry and sends the slave into the city streets to "bring in the poor, the crippled, the blind, and the lame" (v. 21). Notice that the first group to be invited included persons of property who could afford to buy land or oxen or to get married. Now, with the feast all ready, the master does not wish to waste it and so decides to do a good deed by feeding the poor. But even the poor do not come in large numbers; for the slave reports, "Sir, what you ordered has been done, and there is still room" (v. 22). The master then says to the slave, "Go out into the roads and lanes, and compel people to come in, so that my house may be filled. For I tell you, none of those who were invited shall taste my dinner" (vv. 23–24). Who would be out there on the roads that late at night? I am glad I was not at the banquet; they have not yet started eating, and the master is angry, and who knows who next may be coming to the table from off the roads?

In another parable (the marriage feast in Matthew 22:1–14), the slave fills up the table with people off the streets as the master has commanded him; but then the master gets angry at one who is not properly dressed (v. 12) and treats him harshly. Why would he be properly dressed? He was among those gathered by the slave to come in and help fill the wedding hall. Those trying to clean up the story and make the master moral say that the master would have had extra clothing, which the poor could put on to be properly dressed; but Jesus' story does not contain this information.

Where is the good news in those parables of the busted banquets? Any dinner party we give is bound to look good by comparison. I learned the good news of busted banquets fifteen years ago when we were getting a new dean at our seminary. I wanted to make a good impression, for deans influence promotion and tenure decisions and control faculty travel money. (I am now a full professor with tenure, but at that time I was simply an associate professor.)

As the dean was coming from Chicago, I called friends there and asked what kind of entertainment she and her husband enjoyed. I learned that they liked to eat out at fine restaurants and that they appreciated French Impressionist art, which the Chicago Art Institute features. So I wrote the dean and invited her and her husband to join my wife and me as our guests for lunch in San Francisco shortly after they arrived in the Bay Area; and I said we enjoyed eating out at fine restaurants. I added that we would enjoy showing them our favorite museum, San Francisco's Legion of Honor museum, which features Monet and other French Impressionists—who, I noted, were among our favorites. They wrote back accepting our invitation and specifying the day.

As we drove them over the top deck of the Bay Bridge to San Francisco, I knowingly pointed out the prominent sites in the city and then described how a few weeks earlier I had called my good friend the curator at the museum, who assured me the French Impressionist artworks would be on display; for the museum's own collection would be stored soon to make way for a major touring exhibition. (He was not exactly a curator or a good friend; I had met him at a cocktail party, and he worked at the museum.) I described to them the museum experience that lay ahead: how we would walk past a Rodin *Thinker* in the courtyard and then, just inside the museum, see a newly acquired Cézanne *Rocks and Trees.* After that, we would go into the gallery to the right and see the collection of Monet paintings and other French Impressionist art.

We arrived at the museum, walked past the Rodin *Thinker* in the courtyard, opened the front door—and there, where the Cézanne should have been, was a blank wall. I quickly glanced into the gallery to the right and saw other blank walls. All the art had been taken down. "My good friend the curator" had not called me to say that the art was coming down earlier than planned. The dean was no doubt thinking, What friend? Knowing that tenure was now out of the question, but hoping to recoup on the travel money, I suggested we go first to an early lunch and then go to the De Young Museum in Golden Gate Park, which emphasizes American art, my specialty.

A month earlier, my wife and I had had dinner at the restaurant to which we were now heading. While they required reservations for dinner long in advance, they did not take reservations for lunch. One simply arrived and put in one's name and had drinks while waiting to be called to a table. I explained all this to the dean and said confidently that we would get in before the crowd as it was still early. Driving from the museum toward the restaurant, I saw a parking space and pulled right into it. I explained that although we were eight blocks from the restaurant, one rarely found a free parking space on the street and that parking lots charged as much as twenty dollars for just a few hours in this city. I mentioned that the *San Francisco Chronicle*'s humorous columnist, Herb Caen, frequently noted the high price for parking in the city, in contrast to parking all day for twenty-five cents in Oakland, and concluded, "You get what you pay for."

The problem was that they were from the flat plains of Illinois and we were now walking eight blocks up and down the steep hills of San Francisco, and we had passed two other free parking spaces much closer to the restaurant. That gave me time to describe the extensive wine list, the wonderful array of appetizers, and the fine entrees and desserts that awaited us. But when we finally arrived at the restaurant, it was closed for renovation.

Fortunately, I remembered a nearby Greek restaurant named Jackie's and Ari's, which my wife and I had frequented some years earlier, so I explained we would go there instead. As we walked four more blocks, I described some of the hearty peasant fare we could expect at that restaurant, which had few wines but good ones; we arrived to find it had become one of those bad Italian pizza joints serving cardboard pizzas that burn the roof of your mouth. The dean said, "Let us eat here."

As we were having "lunch," I was in speechless despair until I looked across the street and saw a Gellato Ice Cream store. I turned to the dean and said, "This has been a terrible day: no art, and worse than no food; but after we finish here, we are going just across the street to have the best ice cream you have ever tasted. There are not many flavors; but their ice cream has the highest butterfat content anywhere. I know you come from Chicago, near northern Illinois and Wisconsin dairy country; but you have never had ice cream as good as this Italian kind." We finished lunch by twelve noon and walked across the street; but Gellato's did not open until three.

With hardly a word, we walked back to the car twelve blocks away, drove them back to Berkeley, and dropped them off at their apartment. As I drove toward our home, I turned to my wife and said, "I think we can start packing now." But five minutes after our arrival home, the phone rang; it was the dean inviting us over to their apartment for dinner the next night. I responded, "I am so glad you called. After today, I thought I would never hear from you again."

"Look, Doug," the dean said. "We knew what you were doing, for your friends in Chicago had shared with us that you had inquired about our interests." She went on. "Your friends also told us that your wife is a wonderful gourmet cook and you have a cellar of fine wines, so that your dinner parties are spectacular." She then added, "Hearing all that, we were hesitant ever to invite you over for a meal; but after what happened today. . . . "

That was how I learned the good news of busted banquets and why we should tell grandparent stories to encourage people to invite other people over to dinner.

Jesse Helms and Jesse Jackson Together in the White House

The Mind-Boggling Humor of Jesus' Parables

As Jesus dines with tax collectors and prostitutes and keeps a table open to all, his parables include both those people we call good and those we call bad. He takes the human beings we keep separate in our minds, and he puts them together and calls them the kingdom of God. The result boggles the mind and produces humor. Such humor is present in the parables of the yeast, the mustard seed, the lost sheep, the good Samaritan, the friend at midnight, and the workers in the vineyard. In chapter 6, we will see how a similar both/and approach is characteristic of Paul's letters and of grandparent letters, whereas parental letters use an exclusive either/or approach.

For example, Jesus says, "The kingdom of heaven is like yeast that a woman took and mixed in with three measures of flour until all of it was leavened" (Matt. 13:33). We do not immediately see the humor, but for a first-century Jew the type of bread symbolizing the kingdom of heaven was the unleavened bread of the passover Seder service, which the father took and gave to them as they remembered the exodus. One would spend the month before the Passover sweeping out the house symbolically and literally to get rid of any leaven. In the popular mind, yeast—or leaven—had become a symbol of the polluted or immoral life; therefore, one aimed to live the unleavened life. For Jesus to say the kingdom of heaven is like yeast is to say it is like an immoral thing. Perhaps he is going to clean it up? No; for that immoral thing is then taken not by a man but by a woman (who would not even be allowed in a place of worship in first-century Judaism). She then puts it in fifty pounds of pure meal until the whole thing is leavened: that is, until the whole thing is immoral. So the kingdom of heaven is an immoral thing taken by a person not allowed in worship and put into a huge quantity of pure meal until the whole thing is immoral.

A contemporary translation would be to say to your most liberal friend, "The kingdom of heaven is putting Jesse Helms in the White House" or, to your most conservative friend, "The kingdom of heaven is putting Jesse Jackson in the White House." An even more adequate expression of that parable is "The kingdom of heaven is putting Jesse Helms and Jesse Jackson together in the White House." That last formulation would be mind-boggling to everyone who cannot imagine such opposites together. Such a parable makes us think again and broaden our understanding of whom and what God embraces.

The parable of the mustard seed is akin to the parable of the yeast, for just as yeast was considered a pollutant and immoral when one wanted unleavened bread or an unleavened life, so was the mustard shrub considered obnoxious by farmers, for its seeds attracted the birds, who then also devoured the seeds farmers had planted for their crops. In addition, the parable of the mustard seed is a parody of the then well-known parable of the cedar of Lebanon, as John Dominic Crossan has detailed.[1]

The following story demonstrates how to bring this humor of parody to life in a sermon or lecture. Before going off to seminary thirty years ago, I was invited by my home church in Rockford, Illinois, to give the sermon one Sunday. I spent over a hundred hours preparing that sermon, for I knew there would be over a thousand people for the Sunday services; and my sermon would be broadcast across northern Illinois and southern Wisconsin. When I stepped into the pulpit, I fully expected my words to start a great awakening in the life of that congregation, an awakening that would spread across the Midwest and reverberate from coast to coast. You don't remember the great awakening of 1967? Several persons said it was a good sermon, and two people said it helped them. I was greatly disappointed.

I described my great hopes and disappointment in a letter to my former youth minister, who by then was ministering out in Seattle. I wrote, "Bob, what is your standard for successful ministry?" He wrote back and said, "If you are able to help five people in five years, that is successful ministry." I responded by writing, "Five people in five years is only a total of twenty-five people. I don't consider that to be much of a success." He wrote back, "You fool, I meant a *total* of five people. Helping one person a year is successful ministry." He also told me to read the parable of the mustard seed in Mark, not Luke.

By then I was in seminary, where we learned to read the commentaries rather than the Bible, so I first learned that in Jesus' time the Jewish messianic expectation for the kingdom of God was likened to the cedar tree of Lebanon. It is not as great as the redwood tree of California, but a cedar tree is the best you can do in the Near East. Ezekiel had likened the pharaoh and the Egyptian empire to a cedar of Lebanon, where "the birds of the air made their nests in its boughs" (Ezek. 31:6); and the prophet similarly likened the Messiah to the cedar (Ezek. 17:22–23). I liked that parable, for the cedar of Lebanon was sturdy and tall and long-lasting.

Then I read Mark 4:30–32, where Jesus said:

> With what can we compare the kingdom of God, or what parable will we use for it? It is like a mustard seed, which, when sown upon the ground, is the smallest of all the seeds on earth; yet when it is sown it grows up and becomes the greatest of all shrubs, and puts forth large branches, so that the birds of the air can make nests in its shade.

(When reading that text, I gradually raise my right arm from my side to high above my head during the part where "it grows up and becomes the greatest of all," and then I drop my hand down to shoulder height on the word "shrubs.")

For my first sermon, I had hoped for a cedar of Lebanon; but I got a mustard shrub. Jesus' original parable is a parody of the Jewish messianic expectation, just like being born in a Bethlehem stable instead of in a Jerusalem royal court or like riding into Jerusalem on a colt, the foal of an ass, instead of in a splendid chariot drawn by six regal steeds. A mustard shrub is shorter than I am and even less stable. If you put a nest of eggs in its branches, you would end up with a lot of broken eggs, for its branches are insubstantial.

I liked Luke's parable better (Luke 13:18–19). He misses the humor and ends up with a tree and birds nesting in its branches:

> What is the kingdom of God like? And to what should I compare it? It is like a mustard seed that someone took and sowed in the garden; it grew and became a tree, and the birds of the air made nests in its branches.

Luke also adds the person's activity of sowing in the garden. Such work and its results appealed to me, and in my early sermons I likened the kingdom of God to an acorn becoming a mighty oak or like United Airlines, which started out small but grew and became one of the largest.

But Jesus' parable in Mark does not liken the kingdom of God to United Airlines but to Pan American: here today and gone tomorrow. That is the most troubling part of Jesus' parable. It is bad enough that we do not get a tall sturdy tree but, worse yet, a mustard shrub is an annual: it dies at the end of one year. Why does Jesus liken the kingdom of God to an annual?

After I graduated from seminary, my first church as pastor was in San Mateo, just south of San Francisco. High on a hill, that newly built church overlooked the Bay Area; but there had been few plantings around the church. So I went with a committee from the church to one of the nurseries to buy plants. I walked into the nursery, immediately spotted some beautiful plants, and urged that we buy them; but the manager of the nursery said, "You don't want those. They are merely annuals and will be gone by the end of the year. You want to buy these hearty perennials," and he pointed to the opposite side of the greenhouse. He continued, "You buy these perennials, and they will be around your church longer than you are."

I didn't like the way he put that, but we turned our backs on the annuals and bought perennials. Why does Jesus liken the kingdom of God to an annual? (To illustrate the humor, I go and call attention to the faces and arms of some young people in the congregation or class when I mention the annuals; then I go and call attention to the faces and arms of older members when I mention perennials and turn my back on the young people.)

Around that church, there were people who lived in apartment houses on one side and people who lived in private homes on the other side. My first year as pastor, I called equally on both; and a few people from both sides joined the church. But I noticed in the second year that those who lived in apartment houses tended to move away while those who lived in private homes stayed. So, in my second year of ministry I turned my back on those who lived in apartment houses and called only on those who lived in private homes. Why does Jesus liken the kingdom of God to an annual?

I soon learned that it is easier to raise large sums for a once-in-your-lifetime building campaign; people give far less for the annual budget. Why does Jesus liken the kingdom of God to an annual? Also, it is much easier to get a budget for the Bible study group and other adult education; if there is any money left over, we might have a young adult or youth program. Adults stay; but youth and young adults are with us for only a year or two. Why does Jesus liken the kingdom of God to an annual?

I noticed, too, that if someone was in the hospital with a broken leg or some other condition from which they would surely recover and I announced they wanted visitors, many people would join me in a hospital call, where we talked about long-term plans with the patient. But if the person were terminal and I announced they wanted visitors, few people volunteered to go and I was not eager to go myself. Why does Jesus liken the kingdom of God to an annual?

One Sunday I announced a long-term member had just been diagnosed with cancer and been given a month to live, and at her request I invited others to join me in going to see her that afternoon. Only one person volunteered. Why does Jesus liken the kingdom of God to an annual?

That volunteer was the director of the drama group at the nearby college. On the way to the hospital, I turned to him and said, "I am new in ministry; and I am not sure what to say to her. The doctor said she has only a month to live." He responded, "A month! A month! If one of my plays were on stage for a month, it would be a great success!" People in the arts will spend hundreds of hours preparing a drama or a piece of music that may be performed only once. We have much to learn from artists about why Jesus likened the kingdom of God to an annual.

I learned much about annuals and humor from that dying woman as well. After we arrived at the hospital, I lingered at the door to her room until she saw us, invited us in, and said, "Where have you been?" I responded that I did not know what to say. She said, "Just tell me a joke." I could not think of one. Then she said, "This week I'll tell you a joke; and next week, you tell me a joke. At that rate, you'll need only a total of two jokes." Then she told me the following joke. First let me note that this is not a Protestant joke, which usually has some significant social purpose to lay low the idolatrous powers of the day. Instead, this is like the humor of medieval Easter sermons, a humor that Søren Kierkegaard said gives one a sense of freedom from necessity.[2] Such jokes are told just for the fun of it and witness to the playfulness of God.

This is the story she told that day:

> A woman went on the Grand Tour: London, Paris, Rome. Her husband stayed home with Fluffy, the cat, and his mother-in-law. His wife called from London and asked how things were going.
>
> He said, "I am sorry to tell you that Fluffy died."
>
> His wife responded, "That's no way to break the news to me."
>
> He said, "What should I have said?"

She said, "You should have prepared me by saying 'Fluffy is on the roof; and I cannot get him down.' Then the next week when I call from Paris, you could say, 'You remember, Fluffy was on the roof; and I couldn't get him down. Well, he fell and was badly injured; but I took him to the vet, who says there is not much hope.' Then, when I call the next week from Rome, I would be prepared for you to say, 'You remember Fluffy was on the roof and fell and was badly injured. At the vet's, Fluffy died.'"

The husband said, "I should have thought of that."

The next week, the wife called from Paris and asked how things were going. The husband said, "Mother is on the roof."

When I returned to her the next week, I was ready with what is now my favorite joke, which I hope to be able to tell on my own deathbed.

The beloved Dr. Samual Upham lay dying; friends and relatives were gathered about the bed. The question arose whether he was still living or not. Someone advised, "Feel his feet. No one ever died with warm feet." Dr. Upham opened an eye and said, "Joan of Arc did."[3]

Actually Upham said, "John Hus did"; but few people now know that Hus was burned at the stake like Joan of Arc. As a joke often depends upon historical knowledge that is fleeting, many jokes are like annuals. Why does Jesus liken the kingdom of God to an annual?

When I see you in another year, I will not ask you, "How great has your church grown or how many people are coming to your worship or group?" Instead, I will say "Tell me about the one odd bird who has nested in the shade of your ministry this past year." With that, I end the sermon on the mustard shrub.

Like the parables of the leaven and the mustard shrub, the parable of the lost sheep features what first-century listeners would not praise but scorn. In that period, one could not be a shepherd and be a Jew in good standing.[4] Shepherds were notorious for hiding sheep to evade part of their temple tax assessments and for engaging with sheep in other activities about which we will not elaborate. While Moses and David might be respectfully remembered as shepherds from long ago, a first-century Jew would no more invite a shepherd home to share a meal than most twentieth-century Christian ministers would invite prostitutes to Sunday dinner at the parsonage, even if Jesus used to dine with them.

There is humor in Jesus directing the parable to Pharisees in Luke 15:4–6 just after they have said, in verse 2, "This fellow welcomes sinners and eats with them." Jesus addresses them as if they were shepherds: "Which one of you, having a hundred sheep and losing one of them, does not leave the ninety-nine in the wilderness and go after the one that is lost until he finds it?" (v. 4). The Pharisees self-righteously would be on the brink of blurting out, "We are not shepherds!" The humor would be like my saying to the board of deacons, "Which one of you, having a hundred prostitutes and losing one of them, does not leave the ninety-nine and go after the one that is lost?" It is likely one deacon would self-righteously blurt out, "I am no pimp!" Such insult humor is missing from Matthew 18:12, where Jesus is reported to have said, "What do you think? If a shepherd has a hundred sheep, and one of them has gone astray, does he not leave the ninety-nine on the mountains and go in search of the one that went astray?" In Matthew's Gospel there is no implied accusation that the Pharisees own sheep or are like shepherds.

The whole first part of the parable is a question to which the answer is not automatically "yes." A shepherd leaving ninety-nine sheep is questionable, either in the wilderness as in the Lukan account or on the mountains as in Matthew. What will happen to the ninety-nine if the shepherd goes after the lost one? The humor is caught by a translation I did for a conference of army officers in Korea:

> Which one of you commanding a company, if one soldier goes
> AWOL, does not leave the ninety-nine on the battlefield and go af-

ter the one that is lost until he finds him? And when he has found him, he lays him on his shoulders and rejoices. And when he comes home, he calls together his fellow officers and commanding officers, saying to them. "Rejoice with me, for I have found my soldier who went AWOL."

One captain responded, "My general would say sternly, 'Where are the other ninety-nine members of the company under your command?' and I would end up in the brig!"

The less than exemplary character of the shepherd is reflected in some mystery plays and paintings used in and outside of medieval and Renaissance worship. In the humorous "Second Shepherds Play" of the Wakefield cycle, Mak has stolen a lamb but then pretends it is his wife's new baby[5]; and the ragged demeanor of shepherds is evident in Hugo van der Goes's *Adoration of the Shepherds* (Uffizi Gallery, Florence) or in Fra Angelico's and Fra Filippo Lippi's *Adoration of the Magi* (National Gallery of Art, Washington, D.C.), both from the fifteenth century.[6] The humor in such plays and paintings reveals the affinity of Jesus for those poor in spirit, economics, or ethics. In the play, the shepherd's mixing up of the lamb and the baby brings down to earth and parodies the profound but sometimes too lofty theological understanding of Jesus as the lamb of God. In the art, the baby Jesus is as slightly dressed as the shepherds are, so the nakedness of Christ resonates with the shepherds' naked knees and other body parts, which poke through the holes in their garments.

In the biblical parable, there is not only a question about leaving the other ninety-nine in the wilderness, there is also the questionable behavior of telling friends and neighbors that one has lost a sheep in the first place, for it makes one look incompetent. Another possible humorous implication of the story relates to calling friends together to rejoice, for that could imply a party. If the shepherd brought that sheep home and called his friends and neighbors together to party, what would he serve to the guests, leg of lamb?

Such exuberant behavior is evident also in the parable of the lost coin (Luke 15:8–9). Would you go around telling people you had lost a coin in the first place? If you did call friends together to rejoice, the party would probably cost at least the value of the coin. The humor of such exuberance in both the parables of the lost sheep and the lost coin is evident in the fine parable that Clayton Schmit and Carol Vallely created in my course on biblical humor a few years ago, and which is reproduced here with their permission:

> By mistake a fat lady dropped an M & M into her purse. She frantically dumped out the contents and searched until she found it. Then she gobbled it down.

Having a fat lady as the central figure in the story is like having a woman in the parable of the leaven or a shepherd in the parable of the lost sheep, or, as we will see, a Samaritan in the parable of the one who helped another.

Part of the humor in the parable of the good Samaritan (Luke 10:30–35) is captured in the incongruity of the very title we have given it. Samaritans were people whom first-century Jews hated for what they thought were good reasons. Generations before that time, Samaritans had cooperated with invaders while faithful Jews were exiled; the Samaritans got Jewish land. Samaritans were therefore viewed as political traitors. A few years before Jesus told this parable, some Samaritans took their pack animals into the holy places of Judaism and let them defecate there to show their disdain for Jewish religion, so Samaritans were viewed as blasphemers.

To understand the humorous mind-boggling effect of this parable, we need to bring to mind someone we consider to be politically evil or religiously immoral and then cast that person as the one coming down the road to help us out of the ditch. Students in courses and ministers and laity at conferences have suggested a long list of such persons whom they consider evil from their different perspectives: skinheads, drug dealers, KKK members,

Jerry Falwell and the Christian right, Jesse Jackson and the Christian left, homosexuals, homophobic police, the IRA, militant Northern Ireland Protestants, tax cheats, the IRS, TV evangelists, liberal TV news commentators, male chauvinist pigs, feminists, Israeli military, and Saddam Hussein. Seeing Saddam Hussein as the good Samaritan of the week is mind-boggling to most of us but no more than having Jesus cast a Samaritan as the helping one.

Where is the good news in this? If we see good coming only from those we consider good, there is little hope; for we see very few persons as good. But if we see good coming from those we consider bad, there is great hope, for we see many persons as bad. The news is filled with those we consider bad; so there are vast sources for good news. In dramatizations of the good Samaritan, I have most appreciated the efforts of students at the seminary or persons at churches or church conferences when they have cast as the Samaritan a person they genuinely dislike rather than casting as the Samaritan a person whom others dislike. I remember when some of my students staged the parable on the front steps outside the chapel of our liberal seminary, Pacific School of Religion in Berkeley. After actors playing professors and students had walked by and not helped a fallen person, a limousine drove up. Out stepped a student made up as Tammy Faye Bakker, who tended to the person on the ground and carried him into her limo, which then drove off. At liberal seminaries and churches today, I suggest that Ralph Reed of the Christian Coalition be cast as the good Samaritan. At conservative seminaries and churches, I suggest that Hillary Rodham Clinton be cast as the good Samaritan. Or, best of all, the limo would drive up and out would step Ralph Reed and Hillary Rodham Clinton arm-in-arm to help the fallen.

The parable's humor is enhanced through one detail that is too often overlooked: by having the priest going *down* the road (that is, from Jerusalem to Jericho), Jesus strips him of any justifiable excuse for not stopping to help. If the priest had been going from Jericho to Jerusalem, he could have been justified by Jewish law in not stopping, for he might be about to celebrate worship in the temple. Stopping to help someone not only might delay him from reaching the temple on time but also might pollute him (by touching someone unclean), and then lengthy purification rituals would be necessary before he could serve again in the temple. But he is not on his way to the temple in Jerusalem, he is on his way to Jericho. He is on vacation and still does not help. People would enjoy that feature of the story and often poked fun then as they do today at the uselessness of clergy.

A further smile results from Luke's account of the lawyer who precipitates the telling of the parable. We see the humor when we ask the question, "With whom in the story can the lawyer and other Jewish listeners identify?" Those who seek to be truly righteous cannot be the robbers who beat up the victim, nor can they be the priest or the Levite who do not help; and they cannot be the Samaritan for reasons we have already explained. That leaves them as the beaten victim in the ditch by the side of the road.

The humor is that the lawyer had originally asked, "What must I do to inherit eternal life?" (Luke 10:25). This story responds, "Do not talk about what you can do, for the truth is that you are unconscious in the ditch. The good news is that help is on the way. The bad news is that it comes from someone you hate." If I were in a ditch and Saddam Hussein came down the road offering me a hand up and saying, "Can I help you out of the ditch?" my response would be "What ditch?" or "I am down here doing a study of ditches and do not need any help from the likes of you." The victim, if he had breath and strength, might well have rejected any help from a Samaritan; but notice that in this story, the victim says nothing and does nothing once he has been beaten up. That suggests he is unconscious and so could not resist help even from a Samaritan.

There is more humor in relation to the lawyer. For his second question to Jesus is, "Who is my neighbor?" (v. 29). His earlier citing of the law and his second question show that he thinks of the neighbor as one he is going to help as part of earning his way into eternal life; but in Jesus' parable, the neighbor is the one who helps him. So there is a complete reversal of worldview, which can be compared to a shift from salvation by works to salvation by grace. The end of the story shows that the lawyer has a hard time accepting the role of the Samaritan in the story. When Jesus asks, "Which of these three, do you think, was a neighbor to the man who fell into the hands of the robbers?" (v. 36), the lawyer cannot bring himself to say "the Samaritan" and so says, "The one who showed him mercy" (v. 37).

Like the parables of the prodigal and the great banquet, this story has no ending. Its final line is the offer by the Samaritan to the innkeeper, "Take care of him; and when I come back, I will repay you whatever more you spend" (Luke 10:35). We do not know if the innkeeper will agree or not. As the Samaritan is offering him no profit but only his actual expenses, the innkeeper might say no. He might also say no to getting stuck with a man who has not yet showed any signs of consciousness.

I invite members of a congregation or class to generate several endings so we see clearly that Jesus' parable provides no single conclusion but invites many possibilities; and we have created some insightful ones. In one ending, the victim dies the next day but the innkeeper continues sending monthly bills to the Samaritan, who dutifully pays them, thinking the man is still receiving care. That is a particularly insightful one as many people assume the victim will recover; they would not help someone unless such help would produce long-term positive results. If Jesus told a story where the victim definitely did recover, it might lead to an endorsement of lifeboat ethics: Help those who have a good chance to recover, but do not spend time and energy on those with little or no hope. But Jesus' parable undercuts such lifeboat ethics by showing help being given to one who may die the next day.

In another ending, the innkeeper cares for the victim for a long period and sends the bills to the Samaritan, but the bills come back "addressee unknown."

In one possible ending, the victim does recover but the innkeeper does not mention that the Samaritan has paid his bill and so later collects from the victim in an example of double billing.

In another ending, the man recovers but is horrified to learn that a Samaritan touched him. The innkeeper promises, for a fee, not to tell the victim's wife, for if his wife learns the truth she might never sleep with him again.

In still another story, the victim recovers and is totally transformed by learning that he was helped by a Samaritan. He gets the Samaritan's business card from the innkeeper and risks the scorn of other Jews by going into Samaria to thank him. When he thanks the Samaritan, he meets the Samaritan's sister, and they fall in love. They marry and form a friendship society between Jews and Samaritans; and there has not been any trouble in the Near East ever since. The hyperbole of that ending may blow out of the water any thought of too happy a solution; but anything is possible when there is no ending.

In another ending, the victim recovers but has chronic neck pain and sues the Samaritan for putting him on the pack animal, claiming such an action threw out his back and neck permanently.

In one poignant ending, the victim slowly recovers and then decides to go up to the male courtyard at the temple in Jerusalem to give thanks to God for his recovery. On the way up that road from Jericho to Jerusalem, he sees a beaten-up Samaritan in the ditch and passes by on the other side. That ending resonates with the Jesus parable of the unmerciful slave who was forgiven a huge debt but then goes out and has put in prison a man who owes him a small sum.

John Kiffmeyer wrote a fine rendering of the good Samaritan parable in one of my classes and allows its reprinting here:

> A man was going from Sacramento to San Francisco one day, and some guys on motorcycles held him up. When they had robbed him of his wallet and expensive watch, they beat him up and drove off in his car, leaving him under a freeway overpass.

Now it just so happened that a priest was passing that way. When he saw the poor guy, he stepped on the gas and sped away. The next person on the scene was a seminarian. He slowed down and looked at the man; then he shifted gears and drove off.

Then a young woman drove up in her new Cadillac, and what she saw caused her heart to fill up with human compassion. She got out of her new Cadillac, and bound up his wounds as best she could. Then she put him in the back seat of her new Cadillac and drove him to a nearby hospital. She said to the nurse, "Please take good care of this man I found badly beaten. Take this money, it's the only money I have just now, but you keep track of what he owes; and anything his Blue Cross doesn't cover, I'll settle up with you at the end of the month when I get my next welfare check."

Just before leaving to teach a summer session abroad, I sent that rendering along with other materials to a magazine for which I was editing an issue on biblical humor. When I returned home, the magazine had been published; but they had used the word "car" instead of "new Cadillac" in the three places where we had so carefully inserted it.[7] I called the copyeditor and asked what happened to the words "new Cadillac" which we had inserted three times. She responded, "I noticed that this was a welfare recipient and so changed *new Cadillac* to *car*; for if it were a new Cadillac, the woman would have been a welfare cheat, and such people never would help anyone."

At this point in recounting her comment, I usually throw my notes up into the air in mock despair. Such an experience helps one understand why generations of editors and translators and preachers and teachers have tried to make moral the parables of Jesus; but miraculously, the power of those parables persists in spite of our best efforts to domesticate them.

The title assigned to the parable of the friend at midnight brings together two other incongruous terms akin to the two terms in good Samaritan. A real friend would not be likely to interrupt the man who is already in bed with his family at midnight, especially with an unjustifiable request that may reveal an unethical side of the "friend," who asks for much more than he really needs. Notice that, like the parable of the lost sheep, most of this parable is in the form of a question, as it is told in Luke 11:5–8 in the 1952 edition of the Revised Standard Version:

> Which of you who has a friend will go to him at midnight and say to him, "Friend, lend me three loaves; for a friend of mine has arrived on a journey, and I have nothing to set before him"; and he will answer from within, "Do not bother me; the door is now shut, and my children are with me in bed; I cannot get up and give you anything"? I tell you, though he will not get up and give him anything because he is his friend, yet because of his importunity he will rise and give him whatever he needs.

Would you go to a friend with such a request? If you did make such a request, would the friend act in the way described?

The request is questionable. In the Near East, one loaf of bread is considered a meal for one person. Therefore, the request should be for one loaf, not three. That difference is underscored at the end of the story by the comment "give him whatever he needs" (v. 8), not whatever he asks. The request for three loaves of bread is the equivalent of knocking on the neighbors' door and asking not for a cup of sugar but for the whole five-pound bag. What would we think of a person who knocks on our door at midnight and says, "A friend of mine has arrived; give me a dozen filet mignons and a case of Dom Perignon"? Note that the request seems to concern just the feeding of the one who arrived on a journey and no one else; we may assume that the man arrived unexpectedly, or otherwise there would have been provision made in anticipation of his arrival. The man who makes the request would probably have eaten earlier. So it appears the request for three loaves is an attempt to get more than is needed for the visitor but something also for the man's own larder. (Not all scholars acknowledge the unethical nature of the request; for example, Kenneth Bailey sees nothing inappropriate in it and instead notes that peasants would see as ridiculous the excuses given for not helping.)[8] While one could make the request moral by stretching the terms and seeing a family accompanying the man on the journey, I find that stretch unjustified by the story, which talks of the visitor as one person only (with the request for bread to set before *him*).

I asked classes and congregations to consider contemporary circumstances where a real friend would not interrupt us but a "friend" like the friend at midnight would. We generated the following possibilities. A real friend would know enough not to call during the dinner hour. A real friend would know not to come up to talk in detail about next month's committee meeting when we are about to start the Sunday worship service. A real friend would not come knocking on the hotel door during our honeymoon or vacation. During the one brief break I get while leading an all-day workshop, a real friend would not follow me into the bathroom, open the stall door to where I am seated, and say, "I have just one more question."

To aid individuals and groups in relating their own lives to this parable, I use a method applicable to many parables and other biblical stories. After studying the text through a class session or sermon, this is the culminating exercise. The worshipers are asked to think of aspects in the story that have parallels in their own lives. Then I read the text and pause at those places, for people to speak out (or remember silently) what they have thought of as parallels. Here are a few parts of that reading:

> Who of you who has a friend will go to him at midnight—(what person or group or nation is interrupting our pleasure by coming to ask for something?)—and say, "Friend, lend me three loaves; for a friend of mine has arrived on a journey, and I have nothing to set before him" (what unjustified demand is such a person, group, or nation making on us?), and he will answer from within, "Do not bother me." (What angry or irritated response are we justifiably making to the demand?)

While we might completely disallow a request asked at an inconvenient time and for an unjustified amount, the biblical text indicates that he will be given what is needed: that is, one loaf, not three, even though he may be uncouth and unethical.

That same method may be used with the good Samaritan story, with moments provided throughout that parable to remember where we are wounded or feel abandoned, from whom we would expect help but not receive it, and from whom we would never expect help because we dislike them for good reason because we think of them as bad. This method allows those in a class or congregation to see details of their lives in a wholly new light, which reveals enemies as bearers of good news for us and which transforms unreasonable interruptions into reminders of God's grace.

4

Injustice in Raising Wages, Grades, and Who's in Hell?

The Cutting-Edge Satire of Jesus' Parables

In many of the other parables, a satirical humor revealing injustice becomes apparent when we have members of the class or congregation cast in each role. In the parable of the talents (Matt. 25:14–30), the distribution of the property at the beginning has a cutting edge evident when I hand the amounts to each of three persons: "To one he gave five talents, to another two, to another one, to each according to his ability" (v. 15). The humor of that last phrase is easier for the audience to enjoy if I have given the one talent to a person who can take a joke. Then the parable notes, "The one who had received the five talents went off at once and traded with them, and made five more talents" (v. 16). I stop at that point and ask the person who received the five talents and doubled them at once, "How did you do that? What were you dealing, a little cocaine? A little insider trading?" To double money at once suggests unethical behavior.

The unethical nature of the one who doubled his money overnight becomes more apparent when the master returns "after a long time" (v. 19) to settle accounts. I ask that first slave, "How much money do you have by now?" That person usually responds "ten talents." I respond, "I am not the IRS; you can tell me how much you really have by now in your Swiss bank account." Often the person persists in saying there are just ten talents. Then I argue, "You doubled your money at once; and now the master comes back 'after a long time.' You doubled the five into ten the first night, by the second night a smart person like you would have doubled it again to twenty and by the third night to forty. How much would you have after a long time?" By this time the person understands and says, "Off the record, I have over a thousand," or, "Plenty," or, "How would you like a tip to keep this whole matter quiet?"

The parable includes a satirical treatment of the master as well. We might expect a morally sensitive master to inquire into how the first slave doubled the money even after a long time; he might ask the slave, "How did you double the money?" But this master is not so circumspect and accepts the money with unqualified praise for the slave, "Well done, good and trustworthy slave; you have been trustworthy in a few things, I will put you in charge of many things" (v. 21). In other words, he gives him the Las Vegas territory as well as Reno. His calling that slave "good" and "trustworthy" is another ironic touch in the story and shows that the master may not be too perceptive or too ethical himself.

That the master may be unethical is suggested by the encounter with the third slave. When giving back the talent he had buried in the ground, that slave says, "Master, I knew that you were a harsh man, reaping where you did not sow, and gathering where you did not scatter seed" (v. 24). In that statement, there is an accusation that the master is a rip-off artist: reaping other people's crops. If the master's following response ended in a period, he would be admitting he was a crook; but the master's response ends with a question mark and so is not an admission of the charge but allows the story to be ambiguous. "You knew, did you, that I reap where I did not sow and gather where I did not scatter? Then you ought to have invested my money with the bankers, and on my return I would have received what was my own with interest." (vv. 26–27). In effect, the master says that if the slave thought the master was a crook (the type who would rip off others' crops), the slave should have invested the money with the bankers to earn interest. Earning any interest on money was viewed as usury and is one of the most frequently damned sins in scripture, for it made the rich richer and the poor poorer and so undermined society. The master's final words (vv. 28–30) have that same effect as usury:

> So take the talent from him, and give it to the one with the ten talents. For to all those who have, more will be given, and they will have an abundance; but from those who have nothing, even what they have will be taken away. As for this worthless slave, throw him into the outer darkness, where there will be weeping and gnashing of teeth.

The last line reflects the conventional wisdom that those who have wealth also are blessed by God, while those who have nothing are damned as well.

Where is the good news for the poor in this parable? It reveals that the one who got ahead was unethical and that the master who blesses him is unscrupulous and perhaps unethical himself; so that master is not God. In the Near East, the common people cheer the behavior of the one who buries the coin in the ground; they feel an affinity for him and not for the trader or master, who may be seen as belonging to the merchant class that exploits them.

Jesus' parables often undercut the conventional wisdom, which associates wealth, health, and wisdom with salvation. So the rich man goes to hell while the poor sick man goes to heaven (Luke 16:19–31). It is significant that Matthew does not introduce this parable of the talents by saying "The kingdom of God is like . . ." as he usually does when introducing parables; instead, he says, "For it is . . ." (Matt. 25:14). That could be like a father saying to a son, "Here is the hard way it is going to be in the real world." One may think of the parable of the talents as a foil to the final parable of the last judgment (Matt. 25:31–46), where those who are affirmed as righteous did not think of themselves as saved or know they had done the right thing, while those who are damned thought they were among the righteous and did not know they had failed to do the right thing.

In a conference with clergy and laity many years ago, I shared the foregoing analysis of the parable of the talents; and we

developed the following contemporary rendering, which I repro-
duce with their permission:

> Sam Uncle sent out a letter to his servants. To I. M. Rich he gave
> five tax breaks, to John Middle he gave two tax breaks, to Don
> Low he gave one tax break, and to Mother Striver he gave a trans-
> fer payment. On the following April 15th, Sam Uncle received the
> returns.
>
> I. M. Rich took his five tax breaks and parlayed them into five
> tax shelters. Sam Uncle said, "You did well. You will be tax ex-
> empt for the next ten years."
>
> John Middle took his two tax breaks and found two tax shel-
> ters. Sam Uncle said, "You did well. You will be tax exempt for
> two years."
>
> Don Low reported his income, forgot his tax break, and sent
> his check. He was called in for an audit.
>
> Mother Striver used her transfer payment to feed her children
> and obtained a student loan. Sam Uncle, upon examining her re-
> turn, denied her deduction for educational expenses and declared
> her income (with the loan) in excess of eligibility requirements
> needed for the transfer payment. Sam Uncle subsequently de-
> manded repayment of the transfer payment and garnished her bank
> account.[1]

Several years later, Bill Herzog and I were on our way to an
Oakland A's game and shared similar insights about that parable
of the talents. His fine independent analysis parallels some of the
foregoing thoughts.[2]

Since the talent parable is ambiguous, there are other ways of
looking at it. While not seeing the unseemly sides of the most successful slave and the master who praises him, many have interpreted the parable as praising ingenuity and get-up-and-go and
criticizing those who play it safe. The title appropriate for such a
sermon is "The Lord Loves a Gambler." I think such an interpre-
tation is all the better if one recognizes the rough edges of the successful slave and master. I can imagine Jesus telling this parable

to embrace such unethical characters as sharp traders and unscrupulous masters, whom his own followers disliked as much as
Samaritans. If Jesus could dine with tax collectors who had fran-
chises from Rome to collect taxes but who often ripped off the
people for as much as they could get, he could tell a story including those unethical persons in economic life. Such an interpreta-
tion is good news for the poor in spirit: that is, good news for the
unethical entrepreneurs.

Parables such as the unjust manager and the unjust judge may
have similar good news for the ethically challenged. In Luke
16:1–8, the master and the manager have some similarities to
those in the parable of the talents: "And his master commended
the dishonest manager because he had acted shrewdly" (v. 8). An
additional humorous touch may be seen in the beginning of the
story, where the master has to be told that the manager is squan-
dering the master's goods rather than the master being on top of
the situation and discovering it for himself. The master's reaction
shows equally little acumen. On the strength of the accusation, he
fires the manager without a hearing and without asking questions
about the matter, but he fails to seize the books and "change the
locks" to prevent what soon occurs. Whether the manager was
originally dishonest or just wasteful we do not know, but his reaction to the charge of wastefulness is to say nothing in his own
defense, so we may assume he is not guiltless. His next act is unethical. He goes to those who owe the master money and ingrati-
ates himself with them by altering the books to reduce their debts
"so that, when I am dismissed as manager, people may welcome
me into their homes" (v. 4). This man is especially clever; he does
not falsify the books himself but gets the debtors to change the accounts in their own handwriting. For example, to the one who
owes for a hundred jugs of olive oil, he says, "Take your bill, sit
down quickly, and make it fifty" (v. 6). Because we would expect
the master to throw the manager in jail when he discovers what
has happened, there is humor when we are surprised to hear the
master commend the dishonest man (v. 8).

In one wonderful role-playing of those characters, the master is lazily sipping a drink next to the pool in Florida when he gets a call from a snitch who says his manager is messing up the business. And when the manager calls up the one who owes for a hundred jugs of oil, he uses all his charm—"Hello, Madge! How are the children? You can be justly proud of that bright little Tommy of yours"—and on and on, before he gets to the point of cutting her debt in half, and then he closes with "No need to thank me now. Dinner next week at your place? Oh, that would be lovely!"

In the parable of the unjust judge (Luke 18:2–5), the judge acts much like the master in the parable of the unjust manager: He asks no questions but acts after hearing only one side of the case. Some have tried to eliminate that unethical aspect by saying that an honest widow is a stock figure in storytelling, but in this parable we have only the widow's word that hers is a just cause. The judge decides in her favor just to get her off his back. I think of that parable at the end of every semester, when I give students grades and have some come to my office to argue that the B be raised to an A. Do I sometimes succumb? Will my dean be reading this book?

The two foregoing parables could be good news to the poor or to students with poor grades, for such parables suggest that praise or high marks from masters or judges (or teachers) reflects not one's inherent worth but persistent apple-polishing or browbeating. That those with wealth have not necessarily earned it ethically and may not deserve it can be seen in stories such as the hidden treasure (Matt. 13:44) or the laborers in the vineyard (Matt. 20:1–15). In the former parable, the one who ends up with the land containing buried treasure has acted unethically; for in that day one had an obligation to report to the owner of land any valuables on it before one bought it so the owner received a fair price. And in the latter parable, many of the laborers in the vineyard receive a day's wage for far less than a day's work.

There is further humor in the vineyard parable in the discussion between the master and those he hires at the end of the day, and that humor makes clear that they were not deserving. It is already happy hour when they show up in the marketplace. They were not there earlier or he would have hired them then; for example, those he saw standing idle in the marketplace in the morning, he hired (v. 3), as he did throughout the day. So near the end of the day (the eleventh hour), when he went out and found others standing, his question to them has a satiric edge to it: "Why are you standing here idle all day?" (v. 6). Rather than say they just arrived, they miss the satire and lie, responding, "Because no one has hired us" (v. 7). Of course no one hired them earlier in the day. They were not there to hire.

The satiric view of the rich is evident also in the words put into their mouths and the thoughts put into their heads. For example, in the parable of the rich man and Lazarus (Luke 16:19–31), even after the rich man goes to hell, he persists in trying to order people around, expecting Lazarus to serve him: "Send Lazarus to dip the tip of his finger in water and cool my tongue" (v. 24), and "send him to my father's house—for I have five brothers—that he may warn them" (vv. 27–28). And in the parable of the rich fool (Luke 12:16–20), the landowner's seeming omniscience and elaborate thoughts about what he will do appear ridiculous in the light of what he does not foresee: his imminent death, which will prevent him from doing anything.

In the rich-fool parable, the riches are attributed not to the rich man's brilliance, hard work, or good looks but to the land, which "produced abundantly" (v. 16). All the landowner's subsequent words are merely projections and not actions; for he has done nothing and will do nothing throughout the parable except think about what he should or will do.

> The land of a rich man produced abundantly. And he thought to himself, "What should I do, for I have no place to store my crops?" Then he said, "I will do this: I will pull down my barns and build larger ones, and there I will store all my grain and my goods. And I will say to my soul, 'Soul, you have ample goods laid up for

many years; relax, eat, drink, be merry.'" But God said to him,
"You fool! This very night your life is being demanded of you.
And the things you have prepared, whose will they be?" (Luke
12:16–20)

I use a method called liquid pictures to help us remember the
whole parable and to see the ridiculous nature of the rich man's
thinking. I ask for five people to come forward and give each of
them one phrase from the parable to repeat and accompany with a
gesture or action. For instance, the first person repeats the words
"produced abundantly," with a gesture of growth such as raised
arms; the second person repeats "pull down," while bending over
toward the floor and flailing his arms; the third person repeats
"build larger," with expansive arm gestures moving higher and
higher; the fourth person repeats "eat, drink, be merry" while
miming the guzzling of liquor and swaying drunkenly; and the
fifth person repeats "you fool" and drops to the floor as if dead.
The humor of the juxtaposition is most evident if the first person
says his or her line loudly three times, each time with the accompanying gesture, and then continues to repeat the line more softly
while continuing to repeat the gesture. Next the second person
says his or her line loudly three times, with the accompanying
gesture, and then repeats the line more softly while continuing to
repeat the gesture. The next two persons do their lines in turn,
with gestures. When the fifth and final person drops dead on the
word "fool," the preoccupations of the first four persons' thoughts
and projected actions appear ridiculous.

Jesus gives a satirical visual image of the rich by saying, "It
is easier for a camel to go through the eye of a needle than for
someone who is rich to enter the kingdom of God" (Mark 10:25).
The disciples, who assume that riches are a sign of being close to
God, are amazed and respond, "Then who can be saved?" (v. 26).
Jesus cuts off Peter's comment when that disciple says, "Look, we
have left everything and followed you" (v. 28); Jesus says (vv.
29–31):

Truly I tell you, there is no one who has left house or brothers or
sisters or mother or father or children or fields, for my sake and for
the sake of the good news, who will not receive a hundredfold now
in this age—houses, brothers and sisters, mothers and children,
and fields with persecutions—and in the age to come eternal life.
But many who are first will be last, and the last will be first.

The inclusion of the word "persecutions" in an otherwise positive
list is a satirical strategy aimed at bursting the bubble of the disciples' inflated expectations for riches. (The similar passages in Matt.
19:23–26 and Luke 18:29–30 do not include "persecutions.")

Jesus' beatitudes contain humorous reversals similar to those
in parables. Some scholars, among them John Dominic Crossan,[3]
term them anti-beatitudes. Instead of saying, Blessed are the rich,
Jesus says, "Blessed are you who are poor, for yours is the kingdom of God" (Luke 6:20). As Henry Ward Beecher suggested,
that is one blessing we might rather do without![4]

In Matthew 5:3, the blessing is on the poor in spirit, which is
also a reversal. Usually we would think the blessing would be on
those *rich* in spirit (powerful in prayer, active in worship, and gen-
erous to others); but here the blessing is on those *poor* in spirit
(those who do not know how to pray, never come to worship, do
not give). There is humor also in the second beatitude provided by
Luke 6:21: "Blessed are you who are hungry now, for you will be
filled." We sense the humor when we know that the term translated "filled" is the term for animals eating (*chortazo* in the
Greek): that is to feed or, in today's terms, to pig out. It is not an
elegant term used by the upper class, but a gross one used by the
underclass, as its pronunciation suggests. "Blessed are you who
are hungry, for you will pig out." Such beatitudes have more in
common with the dialogue in *Roseanne* than with the elevated
discourse in a drama on public television.

Similar reversals occur throughout other beatitudes in Matthew.
We usually think the assertive will succeed; but Jesus says,
"Blessed are the meek, for they will inherit the earth" (Matt. 5:5).

At a time when the Roman army occupied the land, the people might think, Blessed are the Zealots, who would rid us of the Romans; but Jesus says, "Blessed are the peacemakers, for they shall be called sons of God" (Matt. 5:9 in the 1952 Revised Standard Version). Few people bless peacemakers, who must be compromisers. The full force of that humor may be sensed if we substitute a former "peacemaker's" name in the beatitude: "Blessed be Henry Kissinger, for he shall be called son of God." I have heard Henry Kissinger called son of a something but never son of God.

Another satirical visual image is directed at those who would lecture others on their problems, a propensity especially of the rich, who assume that having wealth means they have wisdom to dispense. Holding in front of my eyes a bolster from the back of a couch, I wander around, bumping into students in the class or members of the congregation, as I or someone else recites Luke 6:41–42.

> Why do you see the speck in your neighbor's eye, but do not notice the log in your own eye? Or how can you say to your neighbor, "Friend, let me take out the speck in your eye," when you yourself do not see the log in your own eye? You hypocrite, first take the log out of your own eye, and then you will see clearly to take the speck out of your neighbor's eye.

With the bolster in front of my eyes extending outward, so I run into other persons, it becomes apparent that with a log in my eye I not only do not see clearly the speck in another person's eye but do not even see the other person! Sometimes before or after the scripture reading, I walk around with the bolster before my eyes and bump into seated persons, while I make comments such as "I see your difficulty clearly" or "I think my perceptive insights will solve your problem."

To demonstrate how satirical humor directed at the rich may be shared in a sermon or lecture, let me describe my presentation on the parable of the unmerciful slave (Matt. 18:21–35) and how it is a mirror of identity—for Peter, who asks the question that provokes the parable, and for us, who have received help from many but then have spoken harshly of welfare recipients. Reading that text as the gospel before this sermon or lecture, I go toward a man in front and grasp him by the shirt collar, when the servant who has been forgiven seizes another servant by the throat and says "Pay what you owe" in verse 28; and I repeat that same action with the same person whenever I return to that phrase in my sermon or lecture.

Why the anger? Whenever I read that passage, I am struck by the anger of one who's just been forgiven a ten-million-dollar debt. When he comes out after that, what would we expect to happen? In the story, he comes out and takes a person by the throat and says, "Pay what you owe." I would not expect that, would you? He has just been relieved of paying ten million dollars. You would expect him to come out and say, "I have just been forgiven ten million dollars! I feel great and grateful. You don't have to worry about that fifteen dollars you owe me. Forget it. The least I can do in gratitude for all I have been forgiven is to forgive *you* that small sum." Or, recognizing how self-concerned we can be, we might expect him to come out and say, "What a relief! I have just been forgiven a ten-million-dollar debt. By the way, you are not forgetting that fifteen dollars you owe me, are you? No need to pay it right now; next week will be soon enough." But I am puzzled to have him come out, having just been forgiven a ten-million-dollar debt, and come over and grab the man by the throat and say, "Pay what you owe," and have him thrown in jail for owing only fifteen dollars. Why that harsh and angry action?

What if we saw only the end of the story? We see him seizing the man by the throat and saying, "Pay what you owe." What would we think of the one who is treating the other so harshly? He must be someone who always pays his own debts, right? Isn't that why he is angry? His anger is saying, "Pay what you owe, as I always do." That is what the angry harsh treatment would have us think, but it is not true. When I come home and say angrily, "These students are not doing good work in their papers," my wife is wise enough to say, "Chapter 3 is not going well?" When I come home and say happily, "These students are doing fine work," my wife responds, "The publisher accepted your new book?"

The unmerciful slave mirrors Peter's anger, which is expressed just before the parable is related. Peter asks, "Lord, if another member of the church sins against me, how often should I forgive? As many as seven times?" (v. 21). What question should Peter be asking? He might more appropriately ask, "How many times will you forgive my sins?" But Peter's question implies that he himself is sinned against but not sinning. Jesus responds, "Not seven times, but, I tell you, seventy-seven" (v. 22). Then the parable is told. The unmerciful slave's angry treatment of the one who owes him fifteen dollars implies that the unmerciful one has never defaulted on a debt and so mirrors both the anger and the assertion of self-righteousness we saw in Peter's question.

With a Bible study group, I shared my puzzlement over that unmerciful slave's anger and we talked about where we see that type of anger in our own lives. This is not the anger of the poor but the anger of one who can afford ten million dollars of debt. Poor persons cannot be that much in debt; only affluent persons have such debts. The slave was a person of property, as the story indicates by noting that, before he was forgiven the debt, the master was ordering "him to be sold, together with his wife and children and all his possessions, and payment to be made" (v. 25). We decided that we affluent persons expressed such anger most often when talking about welfare recipients.

When talking about welfare, we usually do not speak softly, saying, "We ought to make some changes in the system to make it work better." Our tone of voice usually is an angry one; we say, "These welfare recipients ought to work for what they get." As we talked about these matters, one wealthy member of the church blurted out, "If parents don't work, I think we ought to take away their children." We were startled and asked, "Do you really think that?" He said, "Oh, no. I don't know why I said that." Many of us will admit that when we are in a grocery store line, we feel anger at somebody ahead in the line who is paying with food stamps. We get angry, even though we know that the program was adopted not so much to feed the hungry as to sell more farm products.

Then our Bible study group started discussing when we were angry at welfare recipients. The fellow who had said he would take their children explained that he became most angry at welfare recipients when his mother came to visit him. She was the only person on earth who would ask him the question, "Well, son, what good are you doing in the world?" His many employees never asked him that, but his mother would. So he got angry at welfare recipients. Why? He said, "My company makes novelty items that frankly the world would do well without." He added, "If I stayed home instead of commuting to San Francisco every day, at least I wouldn't pollute the highways."

An architect who was in that discussion group got mad at welfare recipients when his father-in-law visited, usually at holiday times. Like some architects, his architectural studio was right next to his home, right off the kitchen. He could hear his father-in-law say, "Well, when is Bob going to work?" His wife would say, "He is in there working now." The father-in-law would respond, "Ever since he was a kid he liked to draw, but when is he really going to *work*?" So the architect got mad at welfare recipients.

One high school student said he had gotten mad at welfare recipients for the first time that summer when his grandfather visited from the family's Iowa farm. The high school student was proudly feeling like a self-made man because he had his first job. (He was earning about a thousand dollars that summer while probably eating food worth twice that sum. Have you ever met a self-made man? Check to see if he has a belly button; if he has one, he is not self-made.) But the boy felt he was making it on his own. After watching him leave for work in the morning and return in time for dinner, the grandfather said to the boy, "What are you doing this summer?" The boy responded, "Gramps, I am working full-time." The grandfather replied, "That can't be. You don't leave the house until nearly nine in the morning, and you're home shortly after five. That's only half-time work." As a farmer, the grandfather put in about seventy hours a week. The grandson was working thirty-five hours a week and getting full-time pay for what the grandfather considered half-time work.

All of us began sharing the similar awkwardness of having paid holidays and paid vacations (days for which we were paid but not working). Those of us who were ministers or teachers talked of our paid sabbaticals. Then there were people taking early retirement and being paid extra for doing so.

Many of us work seventy hours a week but enjoy the work and would do it whether paid or not. (Do not tell my school's president that.) Or, like the novelty manufacturer, we are not so sure that our work has major positive results. And so we become angry at welfare recipients, for they receive little for not working while we are paid well while having days off for vacation, holidays, or retirement. Our anger is a way of asserting that our being paid for not working or being paid to do what we enjoy is different from their being paid for not working.

I shared with the group my experience as a seminary student when I worked as an assistant to a long-term pastor at a church of affluent persons like ourselves. We went to high tea one afternoon in the home of a grand dame, who had never worked a day in her life, having inherited her fortune. She reminded me of my grandmother, who was always very kind to me. (The definition of a grand dame was given by Margaret Mead as one who suffered during the Great Depression . . . by having to let go the upstairs maid, but she kept the downstairs maid, the cook, and the butler.)

Soon that grand dame launched into her favorite topic of conversation, which I remembered had also been my grandmother's favorite: attacking welfare recipients. As the maid was wheeling in the tea cart, the grand dame said, "I think anyone who has any money ought to work for what they get." I tried to slip under the tea cart when the pastor turned to her and asked, "And when are you going to work?"

I have no idea how to reform the welfare system—some of you will have better insights into finance than I do—but I would like to eliminate the anger in the discussion about the issue. The anger has grown and is expressed often among those of us who have inherited funds or are receiving fine incomes. It is a tenacious problem, as I found out when we had a couple as house guests. My wife knew the woman from college days and thought she had married a rather nice fellow, but she was wrong. They were to stay at our home for a week, eating our food; but even as I was carrying their bags in from the car he launched into his first attack on welfare recipients.

In between attacks on welfare recipients, he explained that he had just finished his enlistment in the Navy while his wife had been a schoolteacher. Both were now going back to school for graduate degrees; they had some fifty thousand dollars in savings in the bank. He kept attacking welfare recipients. While I argued with him at first, after a few days I changed tactics and tried to find some common ground. In the middle of one dinner, I finally said to him, "Obviously there are some people in the system who cheat. I have this friend in Berkeley who has plenty of money in the bank and whose father is very wealthy, but this friend takes food stamps. I think he should be ashamed of himself." There was a long silence.

Thinking he had not understood what I said, I repeated it. There was another long silence, which his wife finally broke by saying, "Then you might not think much of us, because we're taking food stamps too. When you get out of the Navy you qualify for welfare, including food stamps, so we get all those benefits." It was a delicious moment. I resisted shouting out "hypocrites!" for I value that term too much. A *hypocrite* is one who has high standards but doesn't live up to them. Here we had people with no standards whatsoever. I thought at least we would have peace and quiet for the rest of their stay, but by dessert he was back to attacking welfare recipients again.

Let us see ourselves in the mirror of this parable of the unmerciful slave as Peter should have seen himself in that mirror.

Let us keep before our eyes all that has been done for us. Let us remember all those who have given to us. Make a list of such persons now, on paper or in your mind. Go back early in your life for someone who helped you before you could even remember. Our next-door neighbor was Mabel Waterman. (I do not remember her, but I am told she allowed me to crawl over to her place and take apart her vacuum cleaner when I was only two or three years old.) Write down the name of the Mabel Waterman in your life — a grandparent, a parent, an uncle or aunt, a neighbor when you were in your first three years of life. Then write down the name of some teacher from grade school years. (Miss Tomic was my finest teacher. She taught fourth grade in interesting ways, using drama and other arts. I remember meeting her on the street when I was home from college; she said, "Doug, I am so proud of all your accomplishments. Do you remember me?" At that moment I didn't even remember her name, but she had helped me greatly.) Then add the name of some minister along the way; Bob Bradbury and Joe Cleveland both helped me. Then add a teacher or two, or a friend later in life: Bill Poteat, Pat Sullivan, Anne Scott, Harvey Alper.

How many names do you have on your list. Five or six, as many as seven? How many names should you have on your list? As many as seventy-seven? Let us pray.

Dear God, thank you for all these persons we now remember who have done so much for us. We have been recipients of their gifts of time and care. As we remember these names now, and as we struggle to remember the names of many more whom we have long forgotten, remind us, dear God, that we are all recipients of your welfare. In future days, when we hear or see the words "welfare recipients," remind us of these persons who have cared for *our* welfare. Give us hearts of thanksgiving and take away our anger. In Jesus' name we pray.

A Sack Lunch and Bathtub Wine

The Clowning Humor of Jesus' Miracles

A parent would enjoy bragging about Moses feeding the tens of thousands in all the tribes of Israel for forty years in the wilderness. Only a grandparent would tell about Jesus feeding the five thousand a single sack lunch. Even Elijah managed to feed ten thousand, so those who know their Bible see that Jesus' miracle does not one-up Moses or Elijah; quite the opposite. Moses parts the waters so that tens of thousands cross the sea from slavery to freedom; Jesus stills the waters so a few boats get safely to shore. Moses brings the waters back to drown the armies of Pharaoh and save tens of thousands of Israelites; Jesus saves one man from evil spirits, which then go into two thousand pigs and drown. Jesus' miracles are presented as parodies of the much more powerful miracles performed by others, so that his followers will be disabused of the quest for power; but often the miracle stories reveal his disciples' duplicity, so the readers of the Gospels may see themselves as at least as faithful if not more faithful than most of the original followers.

In the miracles, Jesus and his disciples appear more as clowns than magicians. That clowning humor resonates with the grandparent motifs we have seen in Jesus' parables. If Jesus and the disciples appeared as magicians, the miracles would be like parental stories. Immaculately dressed, a magician stands in complete control in the center of the arena. Each trick exceeds the previous one, to the universal applause of the audience. As he effortlessly performs the magic, we feel weak, stupid, and helpless; we can neither do the magic nor figure out how he does it. But in the miracle stories, Jesus gets his hands dirty, gives the spotlight and credit to others, is thanked by few, and is asked to leave town. Jesus appears more like the clown who prefers to interact with individual persons on the sidelines rather than in the center ring, who does unspectacular acts of kindness, and who receives little applause, finally being chased out of the arena by the ringmaster. The clown may try a magic trick but he is clearly not in control, often stumbling and getting his hands dirty, and he cannot do the magic alone. As the clown asks help from a child, who works the magic trick for which the clown takes no credit, we feel strong, wise, and helpful — as we do when reading the Gospels.

To see humor in the stories of Jesus' miracles, look for the rough edges of each story as well as the wider context. The humor is in the dirtiness of the miracle and in the unexpected negative ending, characterized more by criticism than applause; in the poor quality of Jesus' miracle, compared to the achievements of earlier biblical characters and the Greco-Roman miracle workers; in the declining productivity of Jesus' miracles; and in the disciples' duplicity and foolishness. Before looking extensively at the more apparent humor of miracles in Mark's Gospel, I will discuss some miracles in John's Gospel, where the humor has often been overlooked.

In *The Marriage Feast at Cana* (c.1303–1305) in Padua's Scrovegni Chapel, Renaissance artist Giotto di Bondone (1276–1337) revealed his insight into the humor of John 2:1–11. Creating a visual pun, Giotto painted the steward with a belly the same shape as the bulging stone jars in the foreground. The steward appears to have eaten and drunk much too much, and a figure to his left steadies him. The steward is shown as a person on whom one would not rely.[1]

Giotto's art leads us to reread the text and note several clues to its humor. Three hints appear in the number, size, and nature of the stone water jars in which the wine was made. That there were six jars rather than the perfect number seven should alert the reader that this story deals with something other than a glorious ideal. There is hyperbole in the amount created; each of the containers holds 20 to 30 gallons, so there is a total of 120 to 180 gallons. That would equal 50 to 75 cases or 600 to 900 bottles of wine. In our homes, what container do we see that holds 20 to 30 gallons of water? The containers in which the wine was created were used for Jewish rites of purification. Humor is seen when we realize that the story may concern the creation of 120 to 180 gallons of bathtub wine.

Someone missing the humor may assert that the story declares that the wine was the best, but the story says only that the steward *pronounced* the wine to be the best. How would he know? Even if he were not as drunk as Giotto painted him, the steward would have been in no condition to judge a wine reliably. We may infer that he and the others at the wedding had already consumed wine because the story begins with the statement that the wine gave out and Mary told Jesus they had no wine left.

Wine tasters do not drink wine but take a sip and spit it out, for to drink even a little soon makes one unable to distinguish the various wines' qualities. My wife and I made the mistake of buying a case of Barbera at the fourth winery we visited one day. By that time we sensed little flavor in any wine; but this Barbera came through with a fine, full, mellow taste. Two days later we opened up a bottle of that Barbera at the beginning of a meal and found it was a rough rotgut wine; but if we served it at the end of a party, after our sense of taste had been dulled by drinking a few glasses of good wine, people found our Barbera to be mellow and better tasting than a fine wine whose merits they would no longer have been able to appreciate.

The story gives the reader a signal to beware of the steward's judgment just before he renders it. Verse 9 notes that the steward (once translated governor of the feast) tasted the wine, not knowing its source, though the servants did. They knew the wine came from the bathtubs, those huge stone water jars used for purification rituals. We may imagine the servants poking each other in the ribs and restraining their laughter as the steward pontificated on the wine's merits. If he tried to identify the smell, or "nose" of the wine, one of them might whisper, "Bathtub '29."

The steward is not the only figure at which fun is poked in the story; the disciples were also objects of the humor. We may note in verse 11 that this wine was the first of the signs that led Jesus' disciples to believe in him; so the disciples were humorously revealed to believe on a questionable basis, just as Jesus mocked the ground of Nathaniel's faith in John 1:50, where Jesus said, "Do you believe because I told you that I saw you under the fig tree? You will see greater things than these." Such humor at the disciples' expense early in the Gospel prepares the reader for the ways such disciples act foolishly later. Part of the good news is that the reader (like the servants) is more knowledgeable than either the steward or the disciples, who appear foolish. With disciples such as these, it is possible for anyone to be a disciple.

As a graduate student, I remember the fun of knowing that a senior faculty member would bring two bottles of wine to each party while other faculty members thought he brought only one. Noted as a wine connoisseur, he placed one bottle prominently on the wine table but kept the other bottle out of sight until he could place it inconspicuously at the back of the table. The first bottle so publicly presented was actually an inferior wine; but because he had brought it, his peers thought it must be fine and spent much time praising its smell and taste—like the steward praising the wine at Cana. We graduate students knew that the second bottle was far better and spent our time drinking it and laughing at the faculty members who had been fooled. As a result, we did not idealize most of the faculty but thought ourselves as fit as they were to be faculty—or at least as fit as they were to be wine connoisseurs.

A similar type of empowering humor may occur not only to those who read of the foolishness of the disciples and the steward toward the end of the story but also to those who read of the banter between Mary and Jesus at the beginning. When Mary told Jesus there was no wine left, we might have expected him to send his disciples to fetch some or to go himself; instead he said, "Woman, what concern is that to you and to me? My hour has not yet come" (John 2:4). If my mother asked me to take out the garbage and I said, "Woman, what concern is that to you and to me? My hour has not yet come," she might have responded, "Your hour is closer than you think!" In the story, however, Mary's response shows she took no offense but was accustomed to this type of banter; she tells the servants, "Do whatever he tells you" (v. 5). Such a story is not the stuff of conventional Mother's Day sermons, which idealize the relationship of mothers and sons; but it makes it much easier to live with our imperfect relations between mothers and sons.

Missing the humor, others have interpreted the wine in discussions of emerging early church eucharistic theology or in arguments that an inspirited Christianity had replaced an empty legalistic Judaism. Seeing humor in the story does not necessarily eliminate those interpretations; but the humorous details resonate more with references to wine in other biblical passages, which would encourage all people—servants and readers of the Gospel, not just those of governing rank, such as the steward, or those especially called, such as disciples. Prophets proclaim that "the mountains shall drip sweet wine, and all the hills shall flow with it" (Amos 9:13); and "buy wine and milk without money and without price" (Isa. 55:1).

The humor at Cana may be seen in line with the humor of another miracle story in John's Gospel. At the raising of Lazarus in chapter 11, Martha at first seems to show a lavish concern for Lazarus as she criticizes Jesus for failing to come more promptly (v. 21); but then she refrains from rolling away the stone because "already there is a stench because he has been dead four days" (v. 39). Again, when a flaw is revealed in the faith of a person close to Jesus, the reader is encouraged to know there is hope even for those of little faith. Rather than waving a wand to open the cave and unwrap Lazarus, Jesus asks others to take away the stone (v. 39) and unwrap the graveclothes (v. 44). Michael Moynahan has devised a play that contrasts the magical way in which Cecil B. DeMille would stage the raising of Lazarus and the clownlike way of Jesus.[2]

To miss the humor in the Cana story is to drain it of much liveliness. When graduating from seminary, each of our classmates received a tongue-in-cheek award. I was glad not to receive the citation given to one of our timid, humorless graduates: "He turned water into grape juice." In contrast, Jesus was called a drunkard in the same phrase that criticized him for his inclusive table fellowship: "Look, a glutton and a drunkard, a friend of tax collectors and sinners!" (Luke 7:34; Matt. 11:19). His disciples were similarly characterized as drunks, and even the defense of them on one occasion does not deny they were drunk at other times: "Indeed, these are not drunk, as you suppose, for it is only nine o'clock in the morning" (Acts 2:15). In that defense can be detected an implication that if it had been later in the day they might well have been drunk.

Abstinence and temperance were not common in biblical stories or in church history until relatively recently. The exhilaration of drinking was cited even by John Calvin, who said that the wine of communion was "to foster, refresh, strengthen, and exhilarate."[3] Because the Bible reports Jesus instituting the Lord's Supper with wine and turning water into wine at Cana, nearly all Christian churches used wine in communion until the last half of the nineteenth century, when that century's earlier temperance movement became abstinence as Mr. Welch campaigned to replace wine with his grape juice. Even Methodists did not eliminate wine from the Lord's Table until 1876. (They have recently allowed wine back into communion.) Some leading Methodists, such as the Reverend Edward Taylor of Boston, disparaged grape juice as "raisin water"; Taylor, upon whom Herman Melville based his Father Maple in *Moby Dick,* insisted on bread and wine in communion and advised his congregation against wafers and grape juice: "Cast from this church any man that comes up to the altar with his glue-pot and his dye stuff."[4] Similar advice might be given with regard to the treatment of those who approach the Bible without a sense of humor.

In Mark's Gospel, the first healing is of Peter's mother-in-law. To heal her, Jesus both touches her and raises her (Mark 1:29–31). Note that, to minimize Jesus' physical interaction with women, Matthew and Luke clean up the story, so that Jesus touches her but does not raise her, in Matthew 8:14–15, and neither touches nor raises her in Luke 4:38–39. Biblical passages have given occasion for mother-in-law jokes. In doing a scripture reading of Matthew 10:34–38, Henry Ward Beecher caught some of the potential humor by his interjection after mention of mother-in-law in the text:

> I am come to set a man at variance against his father, and the daughter against her mother, and the daughter in law against her mother in law [which might not require much!]. And man's foes shall be they of his own household.[5]

The touching and lifting of a woman in Mark's Gospel is then compounded in the next miracle, as Jesus touches a leper (Mark 1:41). Jesus' control is called into question in that miracle; for he orders the leper to "say nothing to anyone" (v. 44); but the leper "began to proclaim it freely, and to spread the word" (v. 45). So much for Jesus' power to control others.

The dirtiness motif continues in Jesus' next miracle, the healing of the paralytic (Mark 2:1–12). There is wonderful visual and acoustical humor in the removal of the roof to lower the paralytic to Jesus while he is in the midst of preaching to a crowd surrounding him. As the roof is being removed, imagine the dirt falling down on Jesus and the crowd around him, not to mention the noise made by those at work above. In the roof there would be not only much dirt but insects, and perhaps some other living things as well, that would fall down onto those below. The scene is in marked contrast to the respect we might expect people to show Jesus' preaching.

In dramatizing this miracle in worship or class, we have a person playing Jesus seated in a prominent place, surrounded by others, who press in to listen to every word as Jesus speaks softly; but he continually needs to raise his voice to be heard over the rising crescendo of the racket caused by the removal of the roof; so by the end, he is shouting such beatitudes as "Blessed are the meek!" and "Blessed are the peacemakers!" Those carrying the paralytic make loud noises as they mime removal of the roof and drop large quantities of Styrofoam packing material down on Jesus' head and on those around him.

Another rough edge present in many miracle stories appears in this story of the paralytic. Jesus says "Son, your sins are forgiven" (v. 5), and the scribes respond negatively by saying, "It is blasphemy!" (v. 7). Similarly, there is the negative response to his healing the man with the withered hand on the sabbath; the Pharisees take counsel with the Herodians to destroy Jesus (Mark 3:6). Our expectations that helpful healing actions will result in applause or praise are violated by such negative responses and by so few positive responses throughout the Gospels. Instead of building Jesus a Mayo Clinic and hiring assistant physicians for him in response to his miracles, people often criticize him or ask him to leave town. Such stories are good news if you are ever asked to leave town. At the end of this chapter, we will see how to bring to life the humor of such responses.

In Mark 4:35–41, Jesus stills the waters during a storm that has revealed the disciples' fear and lack of faith. In both Mark's and Matthew's Gospels, Jesus is portrayed as the new Moses, as Edward Hobbs has detailed;[6] but Jesus' small-scale miracles are parodies of Moses' great ones. So readers do not miss the comparison, the healing of the Gerasene demoniac in Mark 5:1–20 includes the unclean spirit's saying that his name is "Legion" (v. 9), which would remind people of a large army; and that legion goes into the pigs who are drowned in the sea (v. 13). Whose legions were drowned in the sea? The people would remember it was Pharaoh's legions who died in that way. The association of the army with pigs is humorous in itself; this satirical reference to soldiers as pigs may have heightened the people's enjoyment of the story at a time when the Roman army occupied their land.

Matthew's Gospel tries to reduce the humor of the parody by lowering the number of the pigs and doubling the number of those healed, as well as by removing "Legion" as the name of the unclean spirits. Matthew has Jesus healing two demoniacs at the expense of many pigs (Matt. 8:28–34). Luke keeps the name "Legion" and only one demoniac, as in Mark; but he reduces two thousand pigs to a "large herd" (Luke 8:26–39). In all three gospels immediately after the drowning, the swineherds went into the nearby city, and everyone came out and asked Jesus to leave their neighborhood. We might have expected them to give him tenure or build him a hospital to heal others; but the negative endings to miracle stories are like the rough edges in parables. The healing good news of such wounded parables and wounded miracles may not be apparent to you when you are thriving; but when you have lost a job (and someday you will, if you have not yet had that pleasure) and have to leave town, you may see the good news of being in the company of Jesus, who was also asked to leave.

Jesus' lack of control in this situation is underscored by the way the healed one does not follow his instructions. Jesus tells him, "Go home to your friends, and tell them how much the Lord has done for you, and what mercy he has shown you" (Mark 5:19); but instead "he went away, and began to proclaim in the Decapolis how much Jesus had done for him" (v. 20). He violates Jesus' instruction in three ways: he goes to a public place and not to his home, talks to the public and not just to his family, and tells what Jesus and not the Lord has done.

In addition there is acoustical humor in that miracle story. New Testament scholar Wilhelm Wuellner shared in my biblical humor course how acoustically we may bring to life the humor in Christ's repelling evil forces. If we make the sounds described by the creatures or actions in the Bible, the humor becomes apparent. Wuellner and I developed this method first in relation to the thirteenth chapter of Revelation as described in the following sentences; but I have used it in relation to the miracle of the demoniac, as detailed in a later paragraph.

In Revelation 13, evil forces are described more and more powerfully, as moving from a leopard to a bear to a lion, which would make louder and louder sounds: from a hiss to a growl to a roar. But they are powerless against the Christ, who appears as a slaughtered lamb that at best weakly bleats *baaa* with its last breath. I read aloud the first eight verses of Revelation 13 and pause at key points for the congregation or class to make the sounds that the imagery in the text suggests:

> I saw a beast rising out of the sea [*loud moans*]. . . . And the beast that I saw was like a leopard [*loud catlike hissing sounds*], and its feet were like a bear's [*loud growls*], and its mouth was like a lion's mouth [*very loud roars*].

I continue reading, with the sounds rising to a crescendo as the beast wins battles and finally the war over all nations. Then, in verse 8, I read that such fierce forces have no power against those whose names appear "in the book of life of the Lamb that was slaughtered" [*baaa, baaa*]. Before doing this exercise, I sometimes audition everyone, to hear who makes the most pathetic *baaa,* and have just that one person make the sound when we come to that point in the reading. The humor of the juxtaposition is more vividly heard if one does a more compact reading of verses 1–2, immediately followed by verse 8.

Similarly, the acoustical method helps us hear the humor in the miracle of the demoniac, whose actions suggest louder and louder sounds in Mark 5:3–9. "No one could restrain him" [*growl*], "the chains he wrenched apart, and the shackles he broke in pieces" [*louder growls*], "howling and bruising himself with stones" [*louder shouts*]. There are louder and louder shouts after each phrase until the crescendo peaks when the unclean spirit says, "My name is Legion; for we are many" [*loudest shouts*]. And then, in verse 13, the powerful spirits "entered the swine [*oink, oink*]; and the herd [*oink, oink*] . . . rushed down the steep bank into the sea [*splash, splash*] and were drowned [*blub, blub, blub*]."

This acoustical method works well with other miracle stories, such as the calming of the storm (Mark 4:35–41), the walking on the water (Matt. 14:22–33), and the catch of fish (Luke 5:1–11). In that last miracle story, the men are already weary from toiling throughout the night without catching anything [MOANS]. When they put out their nets again in response to Jesus' urgings, the nets are so filled that they are breaking [LOUD SHOUTS]. When the other boat comes out to share the fish, both boats begin to sink under the weight of such a tremendous catch [LOUDER SHOUTS]. Understandably, from exhaustion and awe, Peter falls down before Jesus [SILENCE]. At that moment, Jesus says to him, "from now on you will be catching people" [LOUDEST SHOUTS]. Peter would rather just catch his breath and can look puzzled and worried while the congregation or class responds to another cue card expressive of Peter's puzzlement [HUH?].

Peter is the butt of much humor as he impulsively proclaims his faith one moment and reveals his faithlessness almost immediately. In the miracle of walking on water (Matt. 14:22–33), Peter starts to walk on the water to join Jesus but becomes fearful and begins to sink. Jesus points out Peter's lack of faith: "You of little faith, why did you doubt?" (v. 31). We may remember the humor of Peter sinking into the water when two chapters later Jesus calls Peter "the rock": "And I tell you, you are Peter, and on this rock I will build my church" (Matt. 16:18). In Greek, "rock" is a pun on Peter's name (respectively, *petra* and *Petros*). Elton Trueblood sees the humor by calling Peter "Rocky," for Peter "was anything but stable or durable."[7] We might see the term "rock" as reflecting Peter's mind: dense or dumb in misunderstanding (or failing to understand) parables and other teachings. Peter could be called "blockhead."

Understanding that Peter is "Rocky" helps the reader see humor in the parable of the sower. In Matthew 13:5, the seeds that fell on rocky ground sprang up quickly (as Peter often acted impulsively). Then because that soil had no depth in which the seeds could root (as Peter usually had no depth of understanding or faith), the seedlings were scorched and withered away (as Peter withered under the heat of inquiry and went away from where Jesus was being held as detailed in Matt. 26:69–75).

The feeding of the five thousand in Mark 6:35–44 is a continuation of the parallels between Jesus and Moses and also a story revealing the shortcomings of the disciples. Both Jesus and Moses feed people in the wilderness, but Moses feeds tens of thousands for forty years while Jesus feeds five thousand the equivalent of a sack lunch. Some have tried to magnify Jesus' miracle by thinking that the twelve baskets of leftovers were bushel baskets; but the word basket is more likely descriptive of the small pouch in which individuals carried minimal provisions.

Two chapters later, in Mark 8:1–10, Jesus feeds four thousand, but that story (not repeated in Luke) has two humorous purposes.

The first purpose is to reveal the duplicity and stupidity of the disciples and is evident when we see together the material earlier in chapter 6 of Mark and later in chapter 8. In Mark 6:8–9, Jesus instructs the disciples on what they are not to take on their journey to heal others: "no bread, no bag, no money in their belts; but to wear sandals and not to put on two tunics." After an intervening episode at Herod's court, including the death of John the Baptist, the next time we see the disciples they have just returned and should have no bread and no money; but they are caught with at least some bread and possibly a good deal of money as well, so they did not follow Jesus' instructions.

In trying to go away, Jesus and the disciples are soon surrounded by a crowd. The disciples urge Jesus to send the crowd into town to eat; but he says, "You give them something to eat" (v. 37). Robert M. Fowler argues that implicit in the disciples' response (v. 37) is an admission that they have two hundred denarii: "Are we to go and buy two hundred denarii worth of bread, and give it to them to eat?"[8] John 6:7 would make the matter hypothetical and so get the disciples off the hook of disobedience by reporting the response as "Six months' wages would not buy enough bread for each of them to get a little." That response does not admit that the disciples have that much money.

Then Jesus asks, "How many loaves have you?" (Mark 6:38). While the disciples should have none if they had followed his instructions, they report they have five loaves and two fish. John's Gospel tries to clean up this rough edge of the story by saying they got the five loaves and two fish from a boy (John 6:9). The five thousand are fed; and two chapters later they find themselves in the same circumstances. Again Jesus tells them to feed the people; the disciples respond, "How can one feed these people with bread here in the desert?" (Mark 8:4). They did it in chapter 6, so they ought to be able to do it in chapter 8. They are slow learners. This time they are caught with seven loaves of bread and a few fish. Later in chapter 8 there is one more related incident, underscoring how slow-witted the disciples are. They are in a boat, and Jesus says to them, "Watch out—beware of the yeast of the Pharisees and the yeast of Herod" (v. 15). Now they say, "We have no bread" (v. 16). That would have been a smart response in chapter 6 or earlier in chapter 8; now it is inappropriate. The disciples are like the Englishman who understands the joke only the day after it is told.

There are various ways to bring to life the humor aimed at the disciples' duplicity. I contrast two tableaux or frozen sculptures. To juxtapose these most effectively, I train the congregation or class to close their eyes when I call out "curtains down" and to open their eyes when I call out "curtains up." In the first tableau, I stand attentively as Jesus instructs me to go off and take "no bread, no bag, no money"; then I call out "curtains down." A few moments later, when I call out "curtains up," the people see me standing there wearing two robes with several ministerial stoles around my neck, two long thin loaves of French bread stuffed into my shirt so they stick out conspicuously, two flight bags hanging from my shoulders, and a large suitcase in each hand.

The laughter continues as we reveal item by item what we have in the suitcases as indispensable for ministry or ask the congregation or class to share what they would have in their bags, items Jesus probably meant to include in the list of what any evangelist would need. We pull out a huge replica of an American Express card and say, "Don't leave home without it." We pull out piles of current issues of magazines and newspapers and books that some people think are essential reading and call out their titles: *The New York Times, The Christian Century, National Enquirer,* Andrew Greeley's most recent book, Martin Marty's most recent book, and others. Then we have two whole lines of vestments (traditional and contemporary) and put them all on at once. We have maps, insurance policies, Individual Retirement Accounts, date books and calendars, a portable word processor, hair dryer, deodorant, diplomas, toothbrush, guitars, CDs, pocket calculators, and much much more. This way we reveal the absurdity of all the trappings the disciples and we consider essential to ministry.

To involve people more fully and include items that hit home, ask members of the congregation or class the week before to bring indispensable items in their suitcases to the worship service or class that deals with chapter 6 of Mark's Gospel. The suitcases can be brought forward at the offertory or be arranged in the chancel before the service so they become a visual reminder of this miracle story every time we take a trip and see our suitcases.

The second purpose of the two feeding stories is part of the wider pattern of the diminishing productivity of the miracles in Mark's Gospel. William Countryman has detailed this purpose at length.[9] By having Jesus less willing or less able to perform miracles as the Gospel of Mark unfolds, Christianity would be less attractive to those who wish to gain powerful magic at a time when many wanted such power. To feed five thousand in chapter 6 and only four thousand in chapter 8 lets the reader understand that Jesus' miracles are declining.

To underscore that decline, Mark's Gospel immediately follows the feeding of four thousand with the miracle healing of the blind man at Bethsaida (Mark 8:22–26). Jesus had spit on the man's eyes and laid his hands on them; but the first treatment did not work as fully as we would have expected. The man says, "I can see people, but they look like trees, walking" (v. 24). Back to the drawing board! Jesus has to lay his hands on the eyes again before the man sees clearly. By my doing this as Jesus, in a drama with a person in the congregation as the blind man, the congregation sees the humor, especially when the man says "they look like trees, walking" and I have to lay my hands on his eyes one more time.

The denouement of the decline in miracles is when Jesus curses the fig tree in Mark 11:12–14. A magician may sometimes fail in a magic trick, but he never loses his temper. Even when he does not control the trick, he moves ahead in his program as if nothing has gone wrong. To lose his temper—his self-control—is the ultimate undoing of the magician and reveals he is no longer in charge. Such a loss of temper is exactly what happens in the cursing of the fig tree; and when it withers it is the last "miracle" in Mark's Gospel. Jesus is hungry and, seeing the tree at a distance, goes to have some fruit. But finding no fruit, he says, "May no one ever eat fruit from you again" (v. 14). Mark's Gospel has already noted that "it was not the season for figs" (v. 13), which makes it evident Jesus has lost his temper inappropriately; Matthew eliminates that telling line and has the fig tree wither at once (Matt. 21:19). In Mark's Gospel, the tree does not wither at once but has withered by the time the disciples and Jesus pass that way again (v. 20). Robert Grant has elaborated on the inappropriateness of Jesus' action.[10]

A continuation of the humor directed at disciples may be evident in the healing of the Syrophoenician woman's daughter (Mark 7:24–34; Matt. 15:21–28), when we see the conversation of Jesus and the woman in context. In the first part of the chapter (Mark 7:1–23; Matt. 15:1–20), the disciples did not understand Jesus' criticism of the Pharisees; and Jesus was trying to help the disciples develop a broader viewpoint. In Matthew 15:23, just before the conversation between Jesus and the woman, the disciples came to Jesus and said, "Send her away, for she keeps shouting after us." So we see the disciples next to Jesus as he and the woman talk. Jesus' words may be a satirical expression of the disciples' own prejudices, a humor that the woman understands as she responds in kind. Jesus' words then should be seen as being like Archie Bunker's arch-conservative arguments written by the liberal Norman Lear to discredit such prejudicial arguments.

I bring this humor of Matthew 15:24–28 to life by having two fellows as disciples stand on either side of me as I speak Jesus' lines to a woman. Before speaking to her, I ask the disciples, "Just among us guys, what terms did I hear you using when talking about women—and Syrophoenician women in particular? Was it dogs, or a term for female dogs?" They nod their heads. Then, when the woman approaches to ask for help, I say, "I was sent only to the lost sheep of the house of Israel" and the disciples nod approvingly. When she asks for help, I respond, "It is not fair to take the children's food and throw it to the dogs" and the disciples nod approvingly. When she responds, "Yes, Lord, yet even the dogs eat the crumbs that fall from their masters' table," I respond, "Woman, great is your faith! Let it be done for you as you wish," and the disciples look baffled.

With congregations or classes, I share how the endings of Jesus' miracles often had unexpected negative responses. I note how Edward Hobbs likened Greco-Roman miracle stories to television commercials.[11] Bad breath or bad coffee at the beginning of the commercial threatens the love relationship of the man and woman; but after the miracle worker enters with Listerine or Folger's coffee, love comes again and all is well. But Hobbs pointed out that Jesus' miracles do not end that way.

We role-play a husband and wife at the breakfast table, where the bad coffee seems to end the relationship; but Mrs. Olson in the kitchen helps the wife come up with great Folger's coffee (mountain grown), which restores the relationship in a parallel to the Greco-Roman miracle worker. Then we do the coffee miracle the way it would work out in a Jesus miracle. The first part goes the same way: poor coffee, end of relationship, Mrs. Olson in the kitchen with good coffee. The wife serves the good coffee to the husband, and he loves it. But then he asks where it came from; she introduces him to Mrs. Olson; the husband and Mrs. Olson go off to Sweden together, leaving the wife alone in the kitchen.

A final method I use to reveal the humor of the miracles' negative endings also once unexpectedly revealed a disciple's duplicity. This improvisational drama is based on the healing of the ten lepers in Luke 17:11–19. Thank God, Jesus was not thanked by all ten, as it would make us all feel like failures, for how many people thank us? Each spring, my wife and I give ministerial stoles of her making to many of the graduates at the nine seminaries in Berkeley. We give away around seventy-five stoles a year, and we receive perhaps fifteen thank-you notes from the students. If Jesus had been thanked by all ten lepers, we would have given up long ago; but with fifteen thank-you notes from seventy-five people, we are doing twice as well as Jesus did!

I lead a congregation or class in a reunion of the nine lepers who did *not* give their thanks; like Phil Donahue, I go around asking them why they never got around to say thank you to Jesus for healing them. I also have five or six people volunteer to stand up front as judges, scoring the responses much as Olympic judges score a dive or a gymnastics routine. Each judge has a set of ten cards numbered 1 through 10. I tell the judges to give a 10 for an excellent excuse and a 1 for a very poor excuse. Good responses get anywhere from 6 to 9, and poor responses from 2 to 4. As each leper shares his excuse, the judges are to get their cards ready, but I tell them to wait to show the scores until I turn to the judges and say, "On your mark, get set, judge!" and then all the judges raise their cards to show their scores at once. There is much humor in that juxtaposition of scores, for often one judge gives a 10 while the next judge gives a 1.

I start off the reunion improvisation by saying, "It is wonderful to have the Phil Donahue show here at [name of the place we are meeting] for a reunion of the nine lepers who did not say thank you to Jesus. Hello, lepers!" And the group calls out "Hello, lepers!" I continue. "Not all those invited could come. One invitation came back addressee unknown. And another leper wrote back the following: 'I am glad to hear about the reunion, but I cannot come. After our healing, I met a woman, now my wife, whom I never bothered to tell about my having been a leper; and it is a little late now. But say hi to the whole gang.' Hello, lepers!" The people respond, "Hello, lepers!" Then I ask people for their excuses for never thanking Jesus.

People share some very inventive excuses. One person says he was so thankful to Jesus that he wanted to spread the word about Jesus to others and so did not have any time to go back to Jesus, who he was sure would understand. Another person says she was so eager to see family she had not seen for so long that she forgot all about Jesus. Another person says she had such shabby clothing that the first thing she wanted to do was go to the mall and buy a new wardrobe. After the judges score an excuse, I interview each judge briefly to ask why he or she gave that score. Usually the reason for the score reveals the judge's own values. For example, those who give a high score for the excuse about needing a better wardrobe are often well dressed and say they enjoy shopping. To those who give a low score for the excuse about seeing family, I ask, "Don't you love your mother?" A judge who usually gave a high score evoked laughter when he gave a low score, as did a judge who usually gave a low score but in one case gave a high score. To the latter, I inquired, "Do you know that person to whom you just gave a high score?" And he admitted, "She is my wife."

I have only heard one excuse that scored a perfect ten from all judges, and I usually share it at the end of such reunions to climax a sermon or class on the humor of Jesus' miracles. Here is that perfect excuse.

> I did not thank Jesus right away because I followed what he told us to do: to go show ourselves to the priests. After I had done that,

I went back to find Jesus to thank him; but he moved around a lot and had left each place I looked for him. I persisted but never found him; but I did find Peter. I said, "Peter, I am looking for Jesus. Where is Jesus?" And Peter responded, "I don't know any Jesus."

Every judge awarded a perfect ten for that excuse. Thank God for Peter; he makes it possible for each of us to become a disciple.

Love, Grandma

The Fooling Humor of Paul's Letters

I call Paul's epistles "grandmother letters" because they employ strategies that grandparents use in contrast to parents. For instance, most Christmas letters are parental because they brag about the accomplishments of the parents and their children. A parental-style holiday letter would read as follows:

> Mary is at Harvard. Sara is making $400,000 a year on Wall Street. Joan and Phil have a $5,000,000 home in Malibu. The dog won a blue ribbon at the state fair.

In contrast, a grandmother letter is the opposite of a brag letter and more like Erma Bombeck's style of writing:

> Mary is at Harvard for the third time, having flunked out twice. Sara is making $400,000 a year on Wall Street working for Michael Milken at Drexel Burnham. Joan and Phil have a $5,000,000 home in Malibu, but it is slipping into the ocean. And the dog did something; but it is what dogs do. We are trying to get the spot out of the rug.

Whereas the parental brag letter makes the reader feel relatively unaccomplished, the grandmother letter makes the reader feel that his or her life is more hopeful than those described.

Paul's letters are grandmother letters in detailing the failings he and the early churches endured, for a parental letter would have mentioned only the successes. If his letters had described only early church successes, we would give up on our churches today with all their problems; but in light of what Paul writes about the early churches, our churches do not look hopeless. They are at least equally viable.

How can people miss the humor of Paul when he has body parts talking to each other, as in 1 Corinthians 12:15–21?

> If the foot would say, "Because I am not a hand, I do not belong to the body," that would not make it any less a part of the body. And if the ear would say, "Because I am not an eye, I do not belong to the body," that would not make it any less a part of the body. . . . The eye cannot say to the hand, "I have no need of you," nor again the head to the feet, "I have no need of you."

Our perception of the humor increases when we see that Corinthians were behaving like the body parts in the lines of Paul's dialogue.

Corinth was the wealthiest of Paul's churches, filled with many who considered themselves sophisticated leaders—like those body parts that are mostly on the head or the upper part of the body, such as the eye, ear, or hand. Each tried to lord it over the others. Paul's humor exposed the ways they were misbehaving. Many readers expect Paul to be solemn, so they miss the numerous comic elements in his epistles. Paul displays his humorous gifts especially in writing to the Corinthians, because their problems resulted from taking themselves too seriously.

In a time of conflicts at Stanford University, Episcopal priest Phil Wiehe developed that Pauline dialogue among body parts into a refreshing ten-minute play. Persons reading the different parts wore large-sized cutout representations of those body parts. Wiehe elaborated the lines in keeping with Paul's comic direction, so while the eye says to the foot, "If you had some perspective on the matter, you would easily see that the eye is most important to the body," the foot responds, "You are just like all the rest—always looking down on me." When the foot threatens to leave the body, the nose responds, "Good riddance. You smell."[1]

This chapter will reveal many comic elements in Paul's Corinthian letters, as well as ways to bring that humor to life in contemporary education and worship.[2] Later in the chapter there is treatment of the humor in other Pauline letters—Galatians, Philippians, Philemon, and Romans. Rhetorical criticism, which is used increasingly in Pauline studies, helps reveal the humor, for rhetorical criticism details the nature of the mindsets of those to whom each letter was sent and how Paul's comments played with those mindsets.[3]

"I wish you would bear with me in a little foolishness," Paul writes in the opening verse of 2 Corinthians 11. He then details in a grandmotherly way what I call an antiautobiography; it is the exact opposite of the bragging personal histories that informed people's minds in the Greco-Roman world as well as in our own day. We see the humor by contrasting Paul's statements to what we normally read in autobiographies, college and job applications, and *Who's Who* entries. Whereas autobiographies normally brag about fine educational accomplishments (many academic degrees, such as summa cum laude, Harvard), Paul writes in verse 23 that he has had "far more imprisonments" (summa cum laude, San Quentin); while standard autobiographies note how well liked the person is (elected president of the senior class), Paul writes he has received "countless floggings." While most autobiographies boast about physical prowess (excels in tennis and golf and jogs six miles each morning), Paul writes that he was "often near death" (rather sickly, can jog half a block with help).

Verses 25 and 26 continue the parody. Whereas self-congratulatory autobiographies say that the person's praises are sung by one and all with no detractors, Paul writes, "Five times I have received from the Jews the forty lashes minus one. Three times I was beaten with rods. Once I received a stoning." While many autobiographies describe the person's rise as a string of uninterrupted successes, always upward and onward to bigger and better things, Paul writes, "Three times I was shipwrecked; for a night and a day I was adrift at sea."

While autobiographies typically cite the courage and fear-lessness of their writers, who are so strong and well-loved they are oblivious to any danger, Paul says that he has been, "on frequent journeys, in danger from rivers, danger from bandits, danger from my own people, danger from Gentiles, danger in the city, danger in the wilderness, danger at sea, danger from false brothers and sisters."

While the supposed success of many autobiographical writers leads them to say they were richly rewarded and always had a good night's sleep or slept like a baby, Paul notes in verse 27 that he suffered "in toil and hardship, through many a sleepless night, hungry and thirsty, often without food, cold and naked." Finally, Paul writes, "If I must boast, I will boast of the things that show my weakness" (v. 30), and notes penultimate and ultimate things. Often autobiographies end with accounts of accolades awarded to the subject by the kings of the earth. Today, the person would be flown to Washington, D.C., housed at the Mayflower Hotel, driven to the White House in a Lincoln Continental, escorted on a red carpet to the East Room or the Rose Garden, and awarded the Congressional Medal of Honor or other award. Paul writes what at first sounds promising: "In Damascus, the governor under King Aretas guarded the city of Damascus in order to seize me, but I was let down in a basket through a window in the wall" (vv. 32–33). What happened to the red carpet and the award?

Chapter 12 of 2 Corinthians continues this parody of autobi-ographies, which usually ended with a seal of approval from the gods, who confirmed the person's greatness by revealing to him visions of the heavenly plan and divine teachings so he might in-struct humanity. Paul writes of a man being caught up into the third level of heaven, and most scholars believe he speaks of himself; but instead of detailing visions and revelations, he writes (vv. 3–4):

I know a person in Christ who fourteen years ago was caught up
  to the third heaven—whether in the body or out of the body I do

not know, God knows— . . . and heard things that are not to be told, that no mortal is permitted to repeat.

So much for visions and revelations!

Realizing that the Corinthians do boast of their successes, Paul had earlier in 1 Corinthians 4:6–10 treated such successes with sarcasm. In verses 6–7 he hopes

that none of you will be puffed up in favor of one against another. For who sees anything different in you? What do you have that you did not receive? And if you received it, why do you boast as if it were not a gift?

In verse 10, the sarcasm continues. "We are fools for the sake of Christ, but you are wise in Christ. We are weak, but you are strong. You are held in honor, but we in disrepute."

To help contemporary classes or congregations experience the force of the foregoing passages, I pass out brown paper sandwich bags and have the people write on one side of the bags what they are tempted to brag about in their parentlike holiday letters: the ways they feel wise, strong, ethical, and fulfilled like the Corinthians did, as reflected in 1 Corinthians 4:8–10. Then I have them blow up those bags and pop them; for Paul would not have us be puffed up.

On the busted bags, I have them write on the other side their weaknesses, such as the grandparentlike letter from Paul in 2 Corinthians 11:23–12:5: that is, the academic subjects in which they received the lowest grades, the sports in which they do the worst, the times they have been criticized, the times adrift, their sleepless nights, the awards they did not receive, and the spiritual gifts they do not have. I tell them that these grandparentlike stories are the ones they need to tell their children to give them hope. As Paul teaches us, let us not boast except of our weaknesses.

Another humorous grandparent device used by Paul is digression. For instance, in 1 Corinthians, Paul ignores the questions they have written to him until the beginning of chapter 7, where he says, "Now concerning the matters about which you wrote." My grandmother used digression effectively in her letters. If I wrote my parents when I was facing a decision at college—"Should I do this or should I do that?"—they would write back immediately, saying, "Do this." If I wrote my grandmother "Should I do this or should I do that?" she would write back a couple of weeks later, saying, "The dog is well. They are repairing that fence down by the corner where you fell off and knocked yourself out in first grade. Knowing you are at college and do not have time to watch television, here are the most recent developments in *The Edge of Night*." She would then detail for six pages the last six months of episodes, and then on page seven she would say, "Now concerning the matters about which you wrote, this sounds like a good idea and that sounds like a good idea. Love, Grandma." Grandparents affirm "both/and" rather than "either/or" solutions.

By ignoring the Corinthians' questions, Paul punctures the inflated importance they have attached to them. When he finally deals with them (1 Cor. 7:3–4), Paul gives both/and rather than either/or answers: that is, he affirms both contending parties rather than siding with one or the other:

> The husband should give to his wife her conjugal rights, and likewise the wife to her husband. For the wife does not have authority over her own body, but the husband does; likewise the husband does not have authority over his own body, but the wife does.

The humor comes in part from piling, one on top of the last, a whole string of such both/and responses in chapter 7, much as he piles up a whole string of complex questions in chapter 6. The effect is to boggle the mind. It is all the more humorous because Paul's lines introduce ambiguity when the Corinthians want certainty and clarity. Paul also uses mind-boggling imagery, as in verse 18: "Was anyone at the time of his call already circumcised? Let him not seek to remove the marks of circumcision." How would you do that? Very carefully!

To bring out the humor in chapter 7:1–18, I divide the congregation or class into the various contending factions in the Corinthian church and rehearse them to cheer in response to cue cards labeled 1, 2, MEN, and WOMEN. I also have ready a cue card labeled HUH? for use at some points in the reading. I divide the group into two parts, with one side of the room representing those at Corinth who wished to keep Christianity within Judaism. They become Group 1 and cheer whenever I hold up card 1. I help them get into their part by leading them in cheering to the following comments:

> "You are for keeping kosher." Hold up card 1; they cheer.
> "You are for everyone being circumcised, at least all the men." Hold up card 1; they cheer.
> "And you are for everyone getting married and enjoying sexuality and having children." Hold up card 1; they cheer.

Those on the other side of the room represent the Corinthians who wanted Christianity to throw off Jewish traditions. They become Group 2 and cheer whenever I hold up card 2. I rehearse them in this way:

> "You want no more kosher so you can eat whatever you like." Hold up card 2; they cheer.
> "You want no more circumcisions." Hold up card 2; they cheer.
> "You want no more sex." Hold up card 2; a few will cheer while most of Group 2 say nothing or try to move over into Group 1.

I ask them to stay in their role; and I explain that many in this group wanted no more giving and taking in marriage or intercourse, as the world might soon end.

Then I explain that another division at Corinth was between powerful women and powerful men, for this was the most Roman of the Greek cities in which Paul had contact with the churches. A prosperous commercial center, Corinth had women who were Roman citizens and held property in their own right. I rehearse the men in cheering by saying, "Men should be on top!" as I hold up the cue card labeled MEN. Then I rehearse the women in cheering by saying, "Women should be on top!" as I hold up the cue card labeled WOMEN. Then I explain that occasionally Paul says something that leaves everyone responding, "Huh?" and rehearse them by holding up the cue card labeled HUH?

In the following reading, there will be much laughter as the congregation or class members realize how Paul's pithy comments affirm all their juxtaposed ideas and how his strategy does not take too seriously what they thought were ultimate concerns.

The leader reads aloud the seventh chapter of 1 Corinthians and pauses to raise the cue cards as noted in brackets, and the respective groups cheer when their cue cards are raised.

"Now concerning the matters about which you wrote: 'It is well for a man not to touch a woman' [2]. But because of cases of sexual immorality, each man should have his own wife and each woman her own husband [1]. The husband should give to his wife her conjugal rights [WOMEN], and likewise the wife to her husband [MEN]. For the wife does not have authority over her own body, but the husband does [MEN]; likewise the husband does not have authority over his own body, but the wife does [WOMEN]. Do not deprive one another [1] except perhaps by agreement for a set time, to devote yourselves to prayer [2], and then come together again [1], so that Satan may not tempt you because of your lack of self-control. This I say by way of concession, not of command. I wish that all were as I myself am. But each has a particular gift from God, one having one kind and another a different kind [1 and 2].

"To the unmarried and the widows I say that it is well for them to remain unmarried as I am [2]. But if they are not practicing

self-control, they should marry [1]. For it is better to marry than to
be aflame with passion [HUH?]."

At this point Paul may begin telling them more than they
asked (rather like Ann Landers writing back and saying so much
that you wished you had not written and will most likely never
write again!).

> "To the married I give this command—not I but the Lord—that the
> wife should not separate from her husband [MEN] (but if she does
> separate [WOMEN], let her remain unmarried or else be reconciled
> to her husband [MEN]), and that the husband should not divorce his
> wife [WOMEN].
>
> "To the rest I say—I and not the Lord—that if any believer
> has a wife who is an unbeliever, and she consents to live with him,
> he should not divorce her [WOMEN]. And if any woman has a hus-
> band who is an unbeliever, and he consents to live with her, she
> should not divorce him [MEN]. For the unbelieving husband is
> made holy through his wife, and the unbelieving wife is made holy
> through her husband. Otherwise, your children would be unclean,
> but as it is, they are holy [HUH?]. But if the unbelieving partner
> separates, let it be so; in such a case the brother or sister is not
> bound [HUH?]. It is to peace that God has called you. Wife, for all
> you know, you might save your husband. Husband, for all you
> know, you might save your wife.
>
> "However that may be, let each of you lead the life that the Lord
> has assigned, to which God has called you. This is my rule in all the
> churches. Was anyone at the time of his call already circumcised?
> Let him not seek to remove the marks of circumcision [HUH?].

I end the reading there and then ask, "How would you do that?"
The response, "Very carefully!"

With the people knowing their divisions, I go back and dra-
matize the implied dialogue in 1 Corinthians 6:1–20, which is a
long digression away from the concerns the Corinthians have up-
permost in their minds. Paul piles twenty questions one on top of

the other and frames them so the answer to each one is different from the one before.

That strategy confuses the listener, for an audience expects the same answer to each question, as is usual in discourse to build group cohesion. (At a political convention, for example, the speaker may say, "We all here love the human family, don't we?" and the people know to cheer "Yes!"; and he continues, "We all here love our country, don't we?" and the people cheer "Yes!"; and he concludes, "And we are all going to vote for so-and-so, aren't we?" and the people know to cheer "Yes!" no matter who so-and-so is.) By having the answers change from "yes" to "no" to "yes" again, Paul undermines the sense of confidence which any listener might have had and which the prosperous in Corinth (and in our own day) enjoy. Use of long sentences and some double negatives makes it hard to follow. Such a strategy boggles the mind, much as Jesus' parables boggle the mind.

For a Corinthian, who liked to be right, Paul's strategy is disorienting and disconcerting. The implied dialogue is with the mind of the listener, who struggles to supply the right answer but becomes frustrated by the unpredictable pattern, lengthy questions, and double negatives. I stage this dialogue with one person playing Paul reading the questions and with me as a Corinthian answering yes or no, but always giving the wrong answer and correcting myself only after Paul glares at me.

The Corinthian starts out very self-assured and pompous but soon becomes deflated and hesitant. Corinthians thought they were better than other people, so reducing them to a state of uncertainty helped solve their real problem.

PAUL: When any of you has a grievance against another, do you dare to take it to court before the unrighteous, instead of taking it before the saints?

CORINTHIAN: Yes! (*But after he notes Paul's glare, he corrects himself.*) No!

PAUL: Do you not know that the saints will judge the world?

CORINTHIAN: No! (*But then he changes his answer.*) Yes.

PAUL: And if the world is to be judged by you, are you incompetent to try trivial cases?

CORINTHIAN: Yes. (*But then he changes his answer.*) Oh, no.

PAUL: Do you not know that we are to judge angels—to say nothing of ordinary matters?

CORINTHIAN: No. . . . Yes?

PAUL: If you have ordinary cases, then, do you appoint as judges those who have no standing in the church? I say this to your shame. Can it be that there is no one among you wise enough to decide between one believer and another, but a believer goes to court against a believer—and before unbelievers at that?

CORINTHIAN: Yes. . . . No.

PAUL: In fact, to have lawsuits at all with one another is already a defeat for you. Why not rather be wronged? Why not rather be defrauded? But you yourself wrong and defraud—and believers at that. Do you not know that wrongdoers will not inherit the kingdom of God?

CORINTHIAN: Those damned double negatives. No. Yes.
    (*I then have the person playing Paul skip five verses to the next question, in verse 15.*)

PAUL: Do you not know that your bodies are members of Christ?

CORINTHIAN: No. . . . Oh, yes. Yes.

PAUL: Should I therefore take the members of Christ and make them members of a prostitute?

CORINTHIAN: Yes. . . . Oh, no!

PAUL: Never! Do you not know that whoever is united to a prostitute becomes one body with her?

CORINTHIAN: No. . . . Yes? Oh-oh.
(*We then skip two verses to the next question, verse 19.*)

PAUL: Or do you not know that your body is a temple of the Holy Spirit within you, which you have from God, and that you are not your own?

CORINTHIAN: (*He hesitates, cups his hand to the ear near Paul, bids Paul whisper the answer, and then responds.*) Yes.

PAUL: For you were bought with a price; therefore glorify God in your body.

There is other humor in 1 Corinthians. In the first chapter, where those Corinthians who had been previously baptized by Paul might pridefully expect him to greet them by name, as he does in some other letters, he waits until verses 14–16 to note them and then recognizes only a few as an afterthought—a strategy that would deflate any pride felt by those who were trying to lord it over those Paul had *not* baptized.

I thank God that I baptized none of you, except Crispus and Gaius, so that no one can say that you were baptized in my name. (I did baptize also the household of Stephanas; beyond that, I do not know whether I baptized anyone else.)

To help the congregation or class feel the full force of the humor in 1 Corinthians 11–16, I divide them into three groups. The largest group becomes those baptized by Paul, who cheer every time I read the name "Paul." The second group becomes those baptized by Cephas (i.e., Simon Peter), who cheer when I read the name "Cephas." The third group becomes those baptized by Apollos, who cheer when I read the name "Apollos." I rehearse them in cheering to those names, and then I read the following passage. Part of the humor is that they cheer greatly for Paul and Peter and Apollos, but there is silence when the name Christ is read; and the cheering for Paul's name diminishes throughout the reading as those baptized by him sense his strategy to put down their pride.

. For it has been reported to me by Chloe's people that there are quarrels among you, my brothers and sisters. What I mean is that each of you says, "I belong to Paul," or "I belong to Apollos," or "I belong to Cephas," or "I belong to Christ." Has Christ been divided? Was Paul crucified for you? Or were you baptized in the name of Paul? I thank God that I baptized none of you except Crispus and Gaius, so that no one can say that you were baptized in my name. (I did baptize also the household of Stephanas; beyond that, I do not know whether I baptized anyone else.)

Acoustical humor in chapter 13:1–7 treats the Corinthians' central problem of each subgroup insisting on its own preeminence. Acoustical humor is realized when we make the sound that each element in the text would make. I divide the people into various groups mentioned in verses 1 and 2: tongues of mortals (teachers), of angels (choir), noisy gong or clanging cymbal (organist and instrumentalists), prophetic powers (social concern or outreach committee), mysteries (spirituality or prayer group), and so on.

Then, as I read of their part, each group begins speaking out and continues to do so: The teachers repeatedly recite aloud the ten commandments, the choir sings the "Hallelujah Chorus," the social concern committee shouts out the slogans of their favorite causes, the spirituality group chants "Om" or something similar. In this cacophony, I read Paul's words from verses 4–7—such as "Love is not envious or boastful or arrogant or rude. It does not insist on its own way" (vv. 4–5)—as each group continues speaking and insisting on its own way. So we confess our divisions, laugh, and, one hopes, learn to take ourselves a little less seriously.

In a course called Bringing Biblical Humor to Life, I ask students to write contemporary letters based on the humorous strategies in Paul's letters, much as I ask them to write parables based on the humorous strategies of Jesus' parables. One of the best student letters in relation to Paul's first Corinthian letter was this one, written by Suzanne Vargo and used here by her permission.

Paul, called to be an apostle of Frisbee by the will of God. To the Ultimate Frisbee Club, to those who love the game of Frisbee, together with all those everywhere who love the game. Grace and peace to you from God our coach.

I always thank God for you because of the talent God has given you. You have been enriched in every way, in all your throwing and catching and defending. You do not lack any talent as we wait for the end of this great Frisbee game we call life.

I appeal to you, brothers and sisters, that all of you will agree with one another so there will be no divisions among your team. Some have informed me there have been quarrels among you. What I mean is this: One says, "I want to win." Another says, "We should have fun." Another says, "I want to make great plays." And still another says, "Everyone should get a chance to play."

Is the game of Frisbee divided? Should we have one team for the jocks and another for the klutzes? I think not. But we should all play together in love and fun.

When I came to you, I came not as an expert in Frisbee but as a lover of the game. I could not make diving catches. I did not make any amazing plays. But I came preaching joy, and fun, and love for the game. You are not ready for more complicated teaching, for you haven't learned the basics: teamwork.

It is actually reported that one of your members made five long touchdown catches in a row. And you are proud! Shouldn't you rather have been filled with grief? Your boasting is not good.

Now for the matters about which you wrote. It is good to use the large black Frisbee; but sometimes, since some of your members can't throw it as well, use the small green one. And play in

San Anselmo; but for those members who live in Berkeley, play there on occasion also.

Now about athletic gifts, I do not want you to be ignorant. To each is given talent for the team's good. Some can catch well; others throw. Some can make leaping catches; others dive. Some play offense; others defense. All these are the work of one and the same Spirit, and the Spirit gives them to each one just as the Spirit determines.

The team is a unit, though it is made up of many team members. The team is not made up of one member, but of many. If a good defensive player would say, "Since I don't make scores, I'm not a part of the team," he does not cease to be a part of the team. If a good runner should say, "Because I can't catch, I won't be part of the team," she would not for that reason cease being part of the team. As it is, there are many members but one team.

If I made amazing midair catches, but have not teamwork, I am worthless. If I can catch a Frisbee in the end zone with twenty defenders on me, but have not teamwork, I am nothing.

Teamwork is patient and kind, teamwork looks out for all members, teamwork is not self-glorifying but is willing to give up glory for the sake of another. Teamwork always protects, always trusts, always hopes, always perseveres, and teamwork always shares the Frisbee with the weaker members.

I, Paul, write this in my own hand. If anyone does not love the game of Frisbee, a curse be on him or her. My love to all of you. Amen.

Paul often states at length his argument and then briefly states an opposition view, which he then ridicules. We will see how he does that in Galatians 5:1–12 with respect to freedom from circumcision; now we may discern that same strategy in his discussion in 1 Corinthians 14:26–40 with respect to those free to speak in worship. Throughout history, the phrases in that passage have been moved around, with consequent changes of meaning. Verses 34 and 35 about "women should be silent in the churches" have sometimes been placed at the end of the chapter, after verse 40. The phrase in the last half of verse 33 ("as in all the churches of the saints") may be seen as ending the long previous argument about everyone speaking out but in an orderly fashion. Splitting off that phrase of verse 33 and using it as the beginning of the next verse about "women should be silent" gives added authority to those who would suppress women speaking in church.

The argument against women speaking in church may be seen as coming from the Jewish party, which would not have allowed women to participate in Jewish worship. After that argument against women speaking in church (1 Cor. 14:34–35), Paul then in verses 36–38 ridicules those verses 34–35 that conflict with his argument stated in verses 26–33. I bring that humor to life by reading Paul's words (vv. 26–33) and by then having a man stand up in the congregation or class to read what I see as the Jewish argument against Paul's words, verses 34–35. Then I read verses 36–40 as Paul's ridiculing of the Jewish argument.

> PAUL: What should be done then, my friends? When you come together, each one has a hymn, a lesson, a revelation, a tongue, or an interpretation. Let all things be done for building up. If anyone speaks in a tongue, let there be only two or at most three, and each in turn; and let one interpret. But if there is no one to interpret, let them be silent in church and speak to themselves and to God. Let two or three prophets speak, and let the others weigh what is said. If a revelation is made to someone else sitting nearby, let the first person be silent. For you can all prophesy one by one, so that all may learn and all be encouraged. And the spirits of prophets are subject to prophets, for God is a God not of disorder but of peace, as in all the churches of the saints.

> MAN: Women should be silent in the churches. For they are not permitted to speak, but should be subordinate, as

the law also says. If there is anything they desire to know, let them ask their husbands at home. For it is shameful for a woman to speak in church.

PAUL: Or did the word of God originate with you? Or are you the only ones it has reached? Anyone who claims to be a prophet, or to have spiritual powers, must acknowledge that what I am writing to you is a command of the Lord. Anyone who does not recognize this is not to be recognized. So, my friends, be eager to prophesy, and do not forbid speaking in tongues; but all things should be done decently and in order.

The King James Version renders Paul's response in verses 36–38 even more sharply; and sometimes, in response to the man who has spoken verses 34–35, I use that translation.

What! came the word of God out from you? or came it unto you only? If any man thinks himself to be a prophet, or spiritual, let him acknowledge that the things that I write unto you are the commandments of the Lord. But if any man be ignorant, let him be ignorant.

I pointedly read those last lines directly to the man who had read verses 34–35. I believe the foregoing understanding of the verses in chapter 14 is possible, especially in light of 1 Corinthians 11:5, where Paul indicates that women should keep their heads veiled when they pray and prophesy in worship but does not indicate they should *not* prophesy in worship.

In Galatians 5:12, Paul employs a similar humorous strategy in ridiculing those who use Jewish custom and law to argue against him. Earlier in that chapter he argues that Christ has freed us from the need for circumcision (vv. 2–3). While others argued that circumcision was part of the law and necessary for a person to be part of the covenant with God, Paul uses the words "cut yourselves" in a different way; he argues "You who want to be justified by the law have cut yourselves off from Christ" (v. 4). He concludes his argument by saying, "I wish those who unsettle you would castrate themselves!" (v. 12). This carries the opposition argument to a ridiculous extreme: In other words, they say that circumcision is needed to be justified according to the law; why not become more fully justified by cutting off the whole thing? Biblical scholar Hans Dieter Betz has called this "the bloody joke" of Galatians.[4]

Other humor may be sensed when we consider the whole Galatian letter. Expressions that appear harsh when taken out of context may be seen as humorous *in* context. For example, in Galatians 1:8–9, Paul appears to be harsh when saying that an un-named person should be "accursed," but he goes on in the first three chapters to include himself and then Peter and finally all the Galatians in the same boat as the one who is accursed and then adds that Christ has redeemed us from the curse.

I have the congregation or class become the Galatians who have evidently written Paul to ask him to curse out the one person with whom they clash, and I choose a fellow to become the one accursed. Triangulation was alive and well even in that day. Rather than confronting the person directly, these good Christian Galatians try to get Paul to do their dirty work for them. It is like the parishioner who comes up and says, "Very interesting sermon; but I have heard that some people do not care for your ideas. I thought you would like to know."

As Paul, I read verses 8–9 and then invite the people to curse out the one fellow—"let that one be accursed"—and they say, "Curse him." I note that if I end the reading there, it will sound very harsh to that fellow; but the letter does not end there. I go on to read verse 13 and invite the people to curse me—"You have heard, no doubt, of my earlier life in Judaism. I was violently per-secuting the church of God and was trying to destroy it"—and they say "Curse you." Then I summarize the parts of chapter 2, which relate how Peter promised to stand with Paul in his mission to the Gentiles but then would not eat with them. I read Galatians

2:11 and invite the people to curse out Peter—"when Peter came to Antioch, I opposed him to his face, because he stood self-condemned"—and the people say, "Curse Peter." I go to the fellow who was originally being cursed and ask how he feels now. He usually responds, "Much better," or "I have plenty of company."

Then I note that parts of chapter 3 condemn those who are judgmental against others: in other words, the Galatians themselves. The letter explains how those using the law against someone else are finally cursed by the law, which no one can completely fulfill. I read Galatians 3:10 and then invite them to curse themselves—"For all who rely on the works of the law are under a curse, for it is written, 'Cursed is everyone who does not observe and obey all the things written in the book of the law'"—and the people respond by saying, "Curse ourselves." When all have been cursed, I then read verse 13: "Christ redeemed us from the curse of the law by becoming a curse for us—for it is written, 'Cursed is everyone who hangs on a tree.'" I ask the fellow how he now feels, and he responds, "Much, much better." So the cursing of the fellow, which first appeared harsh out of context, has now become full of grace in the context of all three chapters.

A different style of humor is used in the letter to Philemon: Paul uses praises instead of curses to lead Philemon to do as Paul wishes. I have seen that technique used effectively in fund-raising. The minister says something like this: "I thank God for Jim, here, who is known far and wide for his generosity. Because he gives so much, many others give. Without Jim's generosity, many others would give less. But we have no fear; for Jim always gives more than we would ever ask, and even without our asking."

There is gentle humor in Paul's letter to Philemon, but it is powerful. Paul writes, "I always thank my God because I hear of your love for all the saints and your faith toward the Lord Jesus" (v. 4), and "the hearts of the saints have been refreshed through you, my brother" (v. 7), and "Confident of your obedience, I am writing to you, knowing that you will do even more than I say" (v. 21).

While the brevity of dealing with the humor in Philemon is due to the brevity of that letter, I give brief treatment to the humor in Romans because I have not done extensive work on the letter. Central to the humor I see in Romans is the mindset of those who live in the capital or central city of any empire. Bring to mind those persons whom you know in Washington, D.C., or the central city of any region in the country. A superiority is usually found in the minds of those of us who live in such a place. Having spent a year as a postdoctoral Smithsonian Fellow at the National Museum of American Art in Washington, I know both the feeling of being at the center of the action and the feeling that going to nearly any other location would be exile to obscurity. Teaching for twenty years in Berkeley in the San Francisco Bay Area, I sense something of that same feeling of superiority in our students and faculty who wish to stay in the Bay Area.

When Paul writes to the Romans, "I will set out by way of you to Spain" (Rom. 15:28), their pride of place might be deflated at the thought of his visiting them for a brief period on the way to settle in Spain. Spain? That is where you started out *before* fighting up through the ranks of the government or army or business to make it finally to the world headquarters in Rome. It would be like your writing to me at Berkeley, "I will come visit you for a few days on the way to live in Barstow." Or, "I will come visit you for a few days in Phoenix on the way to live in Tombstone." Or, "I will come visit you for a few days in Houston on the way to live in Pecos." Or, "I will come visit you for a few days in Manhattan on the way to live in Hackensack." Or, "I will come visit you for a few days in Chicago on the way to spend the rest of my life in Peoria." Paul will play in Peoria.

Paul writes to the Romans at length about issues that are not central to their concerns (like writing to someone in New York and going on and on about Iowa corn prices); he writes only briefly about the long list of issues they think are ultimately important. To bring the humor of that latter strategy to life, I ask students or worshipers to make a list of the major issues that trouble them: that is, issues akin to the list in Romans 8:35–39. A Roman could no doubt have discoursed at length about any of those more than a dozen items; but Paul gives each one just a fraction of a second. These are important issues; but often we become so exhausted in discussing or worrying about them that we have no energy left to do anything *about* them. The effect of this exercise is to lighten the weight of these matters so we may actually be freed to work on one or more of them.

I read the list from Romans aloud and pause at every item, so each person may think of something from our day to put on his or her list. For "hardship," one might list poverty; for "distress," one might list an issue such as drug use, which, when we read about the problem, increases our sense of stress. For "persecutions," one might list Bosnia, or one of many other countries where there are human rights abuses; for "famine," one might list world hunger. Similarly, one goes through the rest of the list to generate an example in our own day for each issue: "nakedness," "peril," and "sword." I continue the list with the issues in verse 38. While "death," "rulers," and "powers" are understandably on the list, many people are puzzled by "life" and "angels." I interpret those to help people pick out something from their own lives. "Life" is on the list because often a good thing can be taken to excess; so I invite them to put on their lists a good thing in their lives that they may take too seriously. Similarly, an "angel" may be thought of for the purposes of this exercise as some person whom we may tend to idolize too much.

After everyone is ready with a list, I invite them all to stand and shout out as loudly and rapidly as possible every listed item, after I read aloud Romans 8:31–34, which ridicules the idea that anything could separate us from Christ. Their cue to begin rattling off their lists is when I say the first line of verse 35: "Who will separate us from the love of Christ?" Then, as in a race, everyone shouts out the items on their lists and sits down as soon as they finish. The experience lightens the weight of such a list and frees us from being immobilized by worry about the issues; and so may have energy left to work a little on some of them.

I close this chapter with an example of bringing to life the humor in Paul's letter to the Philippians. I tell the class or congregation that Philippians 3:4–8 lists religious achievements in which he used to take pride or consider as marks of his salvation, but which he came to see as of no account compared to Christ's grace. He ridicules these achievements and his reliance on them by counting them as "dung" (v. 8) in the earthy Elizabethan language of the King James Version. (The Greek word *skybalon* means "dung" or other even less acceptable four-letter words.) For the fastidious modern reader, the New Revised Standard Version cleans the word up as "rubbish"; and the New English Bible, among others, translates the word as "garbage," no doubt to be said with emphasis on the second syllable as one raises one's little pinky and sips tea.

To recapture the ambiance of the original Greek, I have people write down on long pieces of toilet paper the parallels in their lives to what Paul has on his list. In verse 5, Paul writes of his religious background and training and morality ("circumcised on the eighth day, a member of the people of Israel, of the tribe of Benjamin, a Hebrew born of Hebrews, as to the law, a Pharisee"). We write down on our respective pieces of toilet paper such items as the church of our baptism, the schools from which we have graduated, and the names of our ethics professors or others from whom we learned morality. Then, in verse 6, Paul speaks of his zeal ("a persecutor of the church; as to righteousness under the law, blameless"). We write down the ethical issues to which we are most committed (e.g., pro-choice or pro-life); we write down the other moral and political causes to which we are dedicated. These may be very helpful causes, but ones we have begun to think of as absolutely necessary. So these issues have become new circumcisions, according to which we judge others as Christian or unchristian depending on whether they agree or disagree with us on any one of these issues alone.

Then I have people hold their pieces of toilet paper up in front of their eyes as I read Philippians 3:4–8. After concluding with the phrase "do count them but dung, that I may win Christ," I say, "Keep that list in hand; and you will know what to do with it in the end."

Role Reversals in Dialogues Between the Finite and the Infinite

Bringing the Humor of Hebrew Scriptures to Life

There is such a vast array of humor in the Hebrew scriptures—and of books studying it—that this chapter will focus instead on methods to bring that humor to life. Among the best recent books on this subject are the comprehensive *On Humor and the Comic in the Hebrew Bible,* edited by Yehuda Radday and Athalya Brenner, and *And God Created Laughter* by Conrad Hyers, whose extensive scholarship in comparative religions allows him to see distinctive features of Hebrew and Christian scriptures.[1] As the unexpected is the basis of much humor, it is helpful to remember what different expectations the different religions held.

Reminding the reader that Babylonian religion, among other religions, held the view that the sun and the moon were each gods in their own right, Hyers's *Meaning of Creation: Genesis and Modern Science* helps us see the humor in the first creation story of Genesis 1, where God is portrayed as creating the sun and the moon. Such a text is like saying, "Nyah-nyah, our God created your gods." In other words, they are not really gods. Formulated during the Babylonian captivity, such a story would be especially enjoyed by the Israelites; they could laugh at those who had enslaved them. Similarly, Hyers helps us see the humor in the second creation story of Genesis 2–3, which was formulated with reference to the period when Solomon and Rehoboam and others took foreign wives and built them places to worship their foreign gods. The story often called "the fall" may be seen as a satirical treatment of such kings and those who followed for all to beware that those foreign gods (represented by the serpent) and those foreign wives (represented by the woman) led the kingdom (represented by the man and woman) to fall and the people to be exiled from Israel (Eden).

Dramatic presentations of biblical humor face the problem of supplying the audience with enough background to see the point without becoming long explanations of it; for such explanations can kill the subject, as E. B. White noted about studies of humor in general. He likened trying to define humor to dissecting a frog, a process in which the subject dies.[2]

I have found the following methods are helpful in bringing biblical humor to life. Presenting a large enough passage of scripture often provides the context as well as the text that is humorous in that context. In that way, the patterns of both sides of a dialogue are more likely to become apparent. In worship, I find it helpful to have two persons rather than just one read a scripture where God and a human being converse. There is inherently a smile in having God and a human being talking with each other, a juxtaposition of the finite and the infinite. That pairing of incommensurates is akin to the humor inherent in a comedy team made up of a tall person and a short person (Abbott and Costello), or a thin person and a fat person (Laurel and Hardy), or a person who acts like an adult and a person who acts like a child (Martin and Lewis).

Genesis 18:20–32 is effectively presented by two readers: one as God and one as Abraham. Role reversal is part of the humor, as Abraham tries to control God and to act therefore like a god, whereas God acts more like a person, showing such emotions as a loss of temper. I make sure to cast as God a person who is able to read angrily and loudly in two places of the text (vv. 29 and 31), as noted by the italicized directions and exclamation points; in that way Abraham's subsequent lines become a chiding of God for becoming angry, especially if Abraham pauses after saying "Oh do not let the Lord be angry . . . " much like a mother chiding a child for an angry outburst.

GOD: How great is the outcry against Sodom and Gomorrah and how very grave their sin! I must go down and see whether they have done altogether according to the outcry that has come to me; and if not, I will know.

ABRAHAM: Will you indeed sweep away the righteous with the wicked? Suppose there are fifty righteous within the city; will you then sweep away the place and not forgive it for the fifty righteous who are in it? Far be it from you to do such a thing, to slay the righteous with the wicked, so that the righteous fare as the wicked! Far be that from you! Shall not the judge of all the earth do what is just?

GOD: If I find at Sodom fifty righteous in the city, I will forgive the whole place for their sake.

ABRAHAM: Let me take it upon myself to speak to the Lord, I who am but dust and ashes. Suppose five of the fifty righteous are lacking? Will you destroy the whole city for lack of five?

GOD: I will not destroy it if I find forty-five there.

ABRAHAM: Suppose forty are found there.

GOD (*angrily and loudly*): For the sake of forty I will not do it!

ABRAHAM: Oh do not let the Lord be angry if I speak. Suppose thirty are found there.

GOD: I will not do it, if I find thirty there.

ABRAHAM: Let me take it upon myself to speak to the Lord. Suppose twenty are found there.

GOD (*angrily and loudly*): For the sake of twenty I will not destroy it!

ABRAHAM: Oh do not let the Lord be angry if I speak just once more. Suppose ten are found there.

GOD: For the sake of ten I will not destroy it.

We sometimes discuss where people find themselves smiling or laughing during that reading. Expecting God to be firmly in control, many are surprised at Abraham's bargaining, and at God's losing control of the bargaining and temper. Some have noted the similarity of God in that passage and Jesus in the miracle stories studied in chapter 5, where Jesus was frequently not in control and at one point lost his temper. Often mentioned is Abraham's lecturing God on justice: how God's initial intentions are not just and what God should do in order to be just. When Abraham says, "Oh do not let the Lord be angry," many remember how their mothers chided them for temper loss when they were children; and they find it humorous that Abraham is correcting God as one would correct a child.

One may employ the same method of using two readers with many other dialogues between God and a human being in Hebrew scriptures: God and Moses, God and Jonah, God and Gideon, God and any of many prophets. One may use the dialogues just as they appear in the scriptures, as just illustrated by the conversation between God and Abraham; or one may move in the direction of elaborating the lines into a longer play. The latter strategy has the virtue of allowing more background material to be integrated; such background material or context is often needed to help persons understand the humor. Several major playwrights have rendered biblical humor in scripts that may be presented in whole or in part. As a sermon, I have created a readers' theater presentation of parts of Paddy Chayevsky's wonderfully humorous *Gideon*.[3] And one may make similar use of Archibald MacLeish's *J.B.*, about Job,[4] or Clifford Odets's *The Flowering Peach,* about Noah.

Brief dramas may also be developed from the dialogues between God and a human being in scripture. Pastor Stephen McCutchan has written a five-minute dialogue between God and Moses and given permission for its use. Many of the words are from biblical encounters between God and Moses, although McCutchan brings together lines that allude to what has happened earlier and what will happen later so as to provide the context as well as the texts.

Because a brief introduction to provide a little more context can enhance our appreciation of the humor, it is helpful to remember some of the encounters between God and Moses. Moses had tried to avoid going to Pharaoh in Egypt by coming up with a long list of reasons why he was the wrong person to send, including "I am slow of speech and slow of tongue" (Ex. 4:10). If we had just that verse in the exchange between God and Moses, we would miss the humor; but the verse is found in a long dialogue where Moses has already amply demonstrated his quick ability to speak (Exodus 3 and 4). So we see that Moses' comment about being "slow of speech" is a lie, but one that God does not buy.

Another clever attempt by Moses to avoid being controlled by God's wish to send him to Egypt occurs in Exodus 3:13–14, where Moses asks for God's name:

> But Moses said to God, "If I come to the Israelites and say to them,
> 'The God of your ancestors has sent me to you,' and they ask me,
> 'What is his name?' what shall I say to them?" God said to Moses,
> "I AM WHO I AM." He said further, "Thus you shall say to the Is-
> raelites, 'I AM has sent me to you.' "

If we know someone's name, we gain some control over that person, as any substitute teacher in high school knows. As long as we do not know the names of students, they are out of control; if we get their names, we can begin to take charge of the classroom. Moses' seemingly innocent question masks his attempt to get control of God. But in response to a request for the name, God gives an elusive response. As that may be translated as either the present or future tense, it is like saying "I will be who I will be" — you will not control me.

Now we are prepared to appreciate more of the humor in Stephen McCutchan's script, "Humor in the Human Situation Seen from Mt. Sinai."

GOD: Moses, I realize that I have said quite a few things these past forty days.

MOSES: You can say that again.

GOD: What?

MOSES: Oh, nothing, I AM. I am really fascinated with all you have to say. I am sure the people are really going to appreciate your giving them all these new rules to live by.

GOD: Moses, you are not being sarcastic, are you?

MOSES: I AM, I am not. I mean, I am not, I AM. Oh, you know what I mean. One thing worries me, though.

GOD: You need not worry, Moses. If you obey all these things I have commanded you, lo, I will be with you always.

MOSES: That is what worries me.

GOD: What's that?

MOSES: Oh, I didn't mean it that way. I mean, you have said a lot of things these past forty days; what if I forget some of them?

GOD: Oh, I am sure you will do fine. Just to help you out, I have prepared a summary statement of my position on these two stone tablets.

MOSES: Gee, thanks a lot. You're sure something lighter, like papyrus, would not serve just as well?

GOD: No, Moses.

MOSES: Well, OK, just thought I would ask. It is a long way down the mountainside.

GOD: I will be with you.

MOSES: Yeah, I know, but sometimes your invisible presence does not seem to carry its share of the load.

GOD: What do you mean by that?

MOSES: Oh, nothing, I—

GOD: *Moses!*

MOSES: What, I AM?

GOD: Look what your people are doing!

MOSES: Uh, I AM, it is a long way down the mountain; I am not able to see as far as you are, I AM.

GOD: Oh, yeah, sorry about that.

MOSES: Besides, what is this "my people" bit? A little while ago they were "your people." Don't forget, I was quite happy tending my sheep in the desert. It was your idea to bring them out of Egypt.

GOD: Moses, when they obey they are *my* people; when they disobey they are *your* people, and right now they are *disobeying*.

MOSES: I am not sure I like those terms, but I am not sure I have any choice. Oh, well, let me have the worst; what are they doing?

GOD: They are building a golden calf! And they are dancing and playing ribald games.

MOSES: Oh, God!

GOD: What's that?

MOSES: Nothing, it is just an expression. It is a little easier than saying, Oh, I AM.

GOD: I see.

MOSES: Listen, I AM. Maybe they are just making a gift for you.

GOD: It is very clearly stated right here in paragraph two: Thou shalt not make unto thyself any graven image.

MOSES: Well, maybe they misunderstood. You know, people don't speak that King James Hebrew anymore.

GOD: Do not make excuses for them, Moses. Yours are a stiff-necked people. Now, therefore, let me alone that my wrath may burn hot against them and I may consume them.

MOSES: Listen, I AM. I do not think that is a very good idea.

GOD: Why not?

MOSES: Well, it is not very good PR, that's all.

GOD: PR?

MOSES: Sure. You have to think of the Egyptian press. I can just see the headlines now: RADICAL GOD LOSES TEMPER, CONSUMES PEOPLE WITH HOT WRATH. Who's going to want to join a community with a God like that?

GOD: I see what you mean.

MOSES: Besides, you know how that Egyptian liberal press is. They are going to dig up all the dirt they can.

GOD: Dirt?

MOSES: Sure. You can just bet that some rabble-rouser will do an in-depth story pointing out how you had made all those promises to Abraham, Isaac, and Jacob and then in a fit of temper broke your promises and wiped them out.

GOD: You're right, Moses. It was not such a good idea. Look, I have a better idea. Why don't you go down and grind that golden calf into fine dust and put it in water and make everyone drink it? That ought to teach them a lesson.

MOSES: OK. Oh, and thanks for the stone tablets. I have just

thought of a great use for them. It is rather dramatic;
but I think it will get their attention.

Dialogues are not the only dramatic arts to bring biblical humor to life. David Steele's poetry helps us sense the humor of
many texts in Hebrew scriptures, including those dealing with
Aaron's attempt to minimize his responsibility for creating the
golden calf. The poem is based on Exodus 32:1–24. The humor in
that biblical text is evident when we compare what Aaron did and
what he later tells Moses he did. It is very clear (vv. 2–5) how cul-
pable Aaron was in creating the golden calf.

> Aaron said to them, "Take off the gold rings that are on the ears of
> your wives, your sons, and your daughters, and bring them to me."
> So all the people took off the gold rings from their ears, and
> brought them to Aaron. He took the gold from them, formed it in
> a mold, and cast an image of a calf; and they said, "These are your
> gods, O Israel, who brought you up out of the land of Egypt!"
> When Aaron saw this, he built an altar before it.

But when Moses asks him how the calf came to be made, Aaron
leaves out many details (v. 24) of what he has said and done to
create it:

> "I said to them, 'Whoever has gold, take it off'; so they gave it to
> me, and I threw it into the fire, and out came this calf!"

The fourteen stanzas of Steele's poem conclude with these two
sentences: "So those who settle for his view/are not at fault for
what they do./They simply follow their desire/and blame the
product on the fire!"[5]

As humor appears when we perceive the whole story and not
just part of it, we chose to develop the following exercise around the
Shechem Covenant in Joshua 24:1–14; for that text includes references to the whole sweep of events from Abraham and Sarah's de-
parture from their homeland, through Moses' exodus, to Joshua's
conquest. Like other grandparent stories, this one includes the

rough edges of references to the people's idolatries and enemies as well as their successes. With the Shechem Covenant, we used the same method described at the end of chapter 3 in relation to the parable of the friend at midnight. I thank William Jacobs for writing up this presentation and giving permission for its inclusion.

We give out the following form during the class or worship or sermon and invite people to fill in each of the seven blanks with single words related to persons or issues from their own lives. After allowing time for them to fill in the blanks, the leader invites the people to rise; the leader then reads the scripture aloud, pausing at each blank to make a sweeping gesture with the hand from left to right across the class or congregation as a signal for them to speak out what they have written. (As they are filling out their forms, I sometimes share with them what I have written down from my life on the blank lines to stimulate their thinking of what they will write down.)

Thus says the LORD, the God of Israel: Long ago your ancestors— Terah and his sons Abraham and Nahor—lived beyond the Euphrates (_____) [*Write in your hometown, for example, De Kalb, Illinois, and call out what you have written when signaled to do so*] and served other gods (_____). [*Write in something to which you gave much of your time in earlier years, for example, Boy Scouts of America. This could be a good thing but one you took too seriously: a former allegiance, idol, or group.*]

Then I took your father Abraham from beyond the River and led him through all the land of Canaan and made his offspring many. I gave him Isaac; and to Isaac I gave Jacob and Esau. I gave Esau the hill country of Seir to possess, but Jacob and his children went down to Egypt (_____). [*Write in some gift or award you have received, for example, a Smithsonian fellowship, or some physical possession you value.*]

Then I sent Moses and Aaron, and I plagued Egypt with what I did in its midst; and afterwards I brought you out. When I brought your ancestors out of Egypt, you came to the sea; and the Egyptians pursued your ancestors with chariots and horsemen to the Red Sea. When they cried out to the LORD, he put darkness between you and the Egyptians, and made the sea come upon them and cover them; and your eyes saw what I did to Egypt (_____). [*Write in one key word or phrase to remind you of some major political or social development, for example, the Civil Rights movement, in the nation or world of our day for which you are thankful to God.*]

Afterwards you lived in the wilderness a long time. Then I brought you to the land of the Amorites, who lived on the other side of the Jordan; they fought with you (_____). [*Nixon had his enemies list; now you have your list. Write in here the name of a company with whom you have had a problem with poor service or a shoddy product or the name of a person with whom you have had problems—an employer or employee, landlord or tenant, or persons or groups in the nation or world whom you see as up to no good.*]

When you went over the Jordan and came to Jericho, the citizens of Jericho fought against you (_____). [*Write in the name of another enemy, for example, Jesse Helms.*]

Also . . . the Canaanites, the Hittites, the Girgashites, the Hivites, and the Jebusites (_____). [*With the Canaanites we are already fighting inside the land; so think of some quality inside yourself that wars against your best intentions, for example, impatience. Once when I did this scenario and swept my hand from left to right for all to speak out their internal enemies, I got all the way over to the right and then heard a late voice from the left saying "procrastination."*]

I handed them over to you. [*In silence, reflect on the fact that you have survived these enemies and idolatries and stand with others who have at least survived. For what purpose? At the end of the silent time, we will close with a responsive reading adapted from the end of the Shechem Covenant.*]

A responsive reading, printed at the bottom of the distributed sheet that contains the foregoing exercise, is done after a period of silence.

LEADER: I gave you a land on which you had not labored.

ALL: We live in a city we have not built.

LEADER: You eat the fruit of vineyards and olive yards that you did not plant.

ALL: Now therefore let us revere the Lord, and serve the Lord in sincerity and faithfulness. Amen.

We have developed many improvisational scenarios to present the contexts as well as the biblical texts and so reveal the humor. For example, having a Phil Donahue-like interview of Abraham and his families allows us to remember the whole cycle of the Abraham stories, even if we are concentrating on only one or two of them on any given day.

With a panel of persons representing Abraham in the middle, Sarah on one side, and Hagar on the other, we see the humor in any self-serving comments that Abraham tries to make. We have Isaac and Ishmael on the panel also. Usually when I ask Ishmael what he thought about Abraham's intention to sacrifice Isaac, Ishmael responds, "That was a fine idea." While Abraham might like to tell selectively only the stories of his faithfulness (his willingness to leave his homeland or his willingness to sacrifice Isaac), the presence of Hagar and Sarah reminds us of his less than honorable conduct (his shabby treatment of Hagar, whom he put out into the desert, and his presentation in Egypt of Sarah as his sister). As Donahue, I interview each character and ask them to comment on one another's observations. One may invite questions from the rest of the class or congregation as the studio audience. A week ahead of time, one may select persons for the panel and have them study the biblical stories; or one may take volunteers from the class or congregation on the spot.

While church curriculum and preaching usually include only a few of the stories about Abraham (the parental stories of moral behavior), the Donahue interview format allows exploration of all the stories (including the many grandparent stories of immoral behavior). With a panel of the five characters just noted, at least one player will have enough biblical knowledge to keep the interview going even if other volunteers have large gaps in their knowledge. By being Donahue, the teacher or minister may focus more of the interview on those who have more to share. Those who say they do not know or cannot remember something often appear to be stonewalling, like White House aides implicated in cover-ups.

For example, when I press Abraham for details about presenting Sarah as his sister to Pharaoh, he often tries to minimize the matter or cannot recall; but usually Sarah can be counted on to tell more of the story. She or I can bring out the facts, which reveal that Abraham was immoral while Pharaoh was trying to be moral. Sarah may say, "When he came down with an illness, Pharaoh figured he had done something wrong. When he saw Abraham and me 'sporting' in the courtyard, he knew we were man and wife. He then confronted Abraham about Abraham's having lied to him and led him into immorality; but Abraham got to leave with many cattle. Did he learn his lesson? We went into another country; and there, to King Abimelech, Abraham said, "I would like to have you meet my sister, Sarah."

Norman J. Fedder has detailed several scenarios we have used over the years of doing workshops together.[6] The Donahue interview format may be used for other biblical stories: for Moses and Miriam and Aaron, or for Adam and Eve and Cain and Abel, for example. Once, doing it with the latter characters, I brought up two persons to interview as Adam and Eve and then brought up Cain as the firstborn. Later, when Abel came up from the congregation and went to sit down, Cain pulled out the chair from underneath him.

Another scenario is the trial where Esau sues Jacob for stealing his birthright. Rebecca appears for the defense, and Isaac appears as a prosecution witness. I cast myself as the judge so I may focus attention on the characters who offer the most insights. The characters may be cast ahead of time, so they can study the biblical texts pertinent to their case. The same format may be used with the parable of the workers in the vineyard from the New Testament, where the ones who worked all day bring a class action suit against the master who paid them no more than those who worked only an hour or less. The parable, which takes only a few minutes to be read, may be shared on the spot, and so the improvisation may be developed without prior study. In the trial scenarios, the class or congregation may become the jury and later discuss and render a verdict.

The reunion format (which I detailed at the end of chapter 5 for the nine lepers who did not say thank you to Jesus) may be used for those who murmured against Moses in the wilderness. We hold a Reunion of the Murmurers and ask them to share why they murmured against Moses. As with the leper reunion, we have judges with cards numbered 1 to 10 to rank the gripes. One of the best gripes I have ever heard given was the following one: "Manna, manna, manna. Baked manna, mashed manna. I just wanted a good steak." That gripe received a perfect 10 from each of six judges; but the seventh judge gave him only a 1. That last judge turned out to be a vegetarian.

I developed an improvisational panel of prophets to discuss issues of poverty and hunger. Amos spoke plainly and boldly on the matter. Isaiah, who was to the manor born, spoke elegantly and proposed that they fly in a fine speaker on hunger for a fundraising luncheon at the Hilton. The differences among the prophets become evident when they are on the same panel, responding to questions from me as the moderator and from the class or congregation. The scenario requires each of the panelists to do advance reading of writings by the prophet he or she represents.

Another scenario involving prophets illumines the humor of Psalms 9 and 10, which may be seen together as a type of self-congratulatory State of the Union address by the leader, who is then interrupted by prophets who use the occasion to call attention to the plight of the poor. The Jerusalem Bible gives the most helpful translation for this scenario and is used in the following paragraphs. To the strains of "Hail to the Chief," I enter as the leader;

my secret service bodyguards cluster around me and evoke applause for me from all the people. I launch into my address (Ps. 9:1–8) and am interrupted by frequent applause and cheers stimulated by my bodyguards. The gist (vv. 3–4) is how everything is wonderful:

> My enemies are in retreat,
> stumbling, perishing as you confront them:
> you have upheld the justice of my cause
> from the throne where you sit as righteous judge.

After a few more such verses, the prophet interrupts the speech by saying (v. 9): "May Yahweh be a stronghold for the oppressed, a stronghold when times are hard."

As leader, I then resume my speech with verses 10 and 11; but the prophet interrupts again with verses 12 and 13, including the lines "he does not ignore the cry of the wretched. Take pity on me, Yahweh, look on my suffering, you who lift me back from the gates of death." I resume my speech with verse 14, but the prophet interrupts again with verse 15: "The nations have sunk into a pit of their own making, they are caught by the feet in the snare they set themselves." Some lines are easy to assign to the leader, other lines are easy to assign to the prophet, while a few lines could be spoken by either one. After a few interruptions, which I as leader barely tolerate by gritting my teeth and smiling somewhat painfully, I send my bodyguards to escort or drag the prophet from the room while the prophet continues to interject the lines of concern for what is wrong, as expressed in Psalm 10:2, "The poor man is devoured by the pride of the wicked, he is caught in the wiles that the other has devised." That is a particularly apt line for the prophet to speak as he is being dragged off by the guards.

We have more than one prophet planted in the congregation, so when the first prophet is dragged off another prophet rises up to continue the interruptions. In a huff, I and my bodyguards may exit while a prophet continues to speak. Once, after my bodyguards had dragged off the last of the prophets, I continued my speech only to be interrupted by one of the bodyguards, who took up the role of prophet!

The final dramatization involves rough humor, which might be introduced after a congregation or class has first experienced the gentler exercises. If proverbs are read by one person directly to another person, the rough humor becomes evident as insult humor. Because scripture readings are often directed to no one in particular, the proverbs' rough-edged humor is missed. I hand out to each person a photocopy of Proverbs 26. Then, as an act of confession, people pair off in twos and take turns reading a verse to each other until they have completed the entire chapter. The first person in the pair reads verse one to the second person and applies to that person the last word: "Like snow in summer or rain in harvest, so honor is not fitting for a *fool*." Then the second person reads the second verse back to the first person: "Like a sparrow in its flitting, like a swallow in its flying, an undeserved curse goes nowhere." Then the first person reads to the second person the third verse and applies the underlined words to the second person: "A whip for the *horse,* a bridle for the *donkey,* and a rod for the back of *fools*." The second person responds by reading the fourth verse, applying the underlined terms to the first person: "Do not answer *fools* according to their *folly,* or you will be a *fool* yourself." The reading becomes more and more acrimonious. It allows the relatively safe expression of aggression, often felt but bottled up inside each of us. Such expression in the context of confession is both honest and humorous, but it is not for the fainthearted. This presentation of Proverbs should not be your first venture into using humor in worship, but it may be your last. Remember Jesus' experience with the swineherds; when you are asked to leave town, you know you will be in good company.

NOTES

Chapter 1. The Prostitute in the Family Tree:
The Telling Humor of Biblical Stories
as Grandparent Stories

1. Augustine, *The Confessions of Saint Augustine,* 31.
2. For examples of Taylor's use of humor in preaching, see Gardner C. Taylor, *The Scarlet Thread;* see also his 1975–1976 Lyman Beecher Lectures, reflecting on preaching as well as including some sermons, *How Shall They Preach?*
3. I created the annotated genealogy in 1971 and published the first version as an article in an issue I edited of *Modern Liturgy* on biblical humor; see Doug Adams, "Bringing Biblical Humor to Life in Liturgy."
4. Jim Groves and Terry Teigen, "Dramatizing Humor in Jonah, Chapter 4."
5. James A. Sanders, *God Has a Story Too.*
6. Robert W. Funk, *Jesus as Precursor,* 74.
7. John Donne, *The Sermons of John Donne,* vol. 2, 154.

Chapter 2. Fractured Families and Busted Banquets:
The Wounded-Healing Humor of Jesus' Parables

1. See James Breech, *Jesus and Postmodernism* and idem, *The Silence of Jesus.*
2. James A. Sanders, "The Ethic of Election in Luke's Great Banquet Parable," in *Luke and Scripture,* 110–11.

**Chapter 3. Jesse Helms and Jesse Jackson
Together in the White House: The Mind-Boggling
Humor of Jesus' Parables**

1. John Dominic Crossan, *The Dark Interval*, 74–77.
2. Søren Kierkegaard, *The Concept of Irony*, 270.
3. Ezra Squier Tipple, *Drew Theological Seminary, 1867–1917*, 136; Halford Luccock, "Research: Human Interest and Humorous Stories of the Church"; Doug Adams, *Humor in the American Pulpit from George Whitefield Through Henry Ward Beecher*, 64.
4. Kenneth E. Bailey, *Poet and Peasant* and *Through Peasant Eyes*, 147.
5. E. Martin Browne, ed., *Religious Drama 2: Mystery and Miracle Plays*, 102–32.
6. Doug Adams, *Eyes to See Wholeness*, 74–75.
7. John Kiffmeyer, "Translating Scripture to Hear Humor," *Modern Liturgy* 6, no. 8 (1978–1979): 7.
8. Kenneth Bailey, *Poet and Peasant*, 124. Bailey described also how the request for three loaves of bread could entail much more, for the bread was used to dip into other dishes, although one loaf per person would be sufficient for such dipping.

**Chapter 4. Injustice in Raising Wages, Grades,
and Who's in Hell?: The Cutting-Edge
Satire of Jesus' Parables**

1. This analysis was written by Genevieve Beagle, Vera Brenner, Dorothy Carlson, Jeanne Fraim, Don Hislop, Clara Jones, Curtis Jones, Lillian Madison, Lucy McGiffin, Jeanne Olson, Dorothy Pease, Allan Pfluger, and Jill Tyler and edited by Doug Adams.
2. William Herzog, *Parables as Subversive Speech*, 150–68.
3. John Dominic Crossan, *Raid on the Articulate*, 75.
4. Henry Ward Beecher, "Bearing One Another's Burdens," *The Sermons of Henry Ward Beecher in Plymouth Church, Brooklyn*, Eighth Series, 1872, 234.

Chapter 5. A Sack Lunch and Bathtub Wine:
The Clowning Humor of Jesus' Miracles

1. This discussion of humor in John 2 appeared as an earlier article: Doug Adams, "Wine and Humor at Cana," *The Fourth R* 5, no. 6 (1992): 7–12.
2. Michael Moynahan, S.J., *Once Upon a Miracle*, 11–24.
3. John Calvin, *Institutes of the Christian Religion*, vol. 2, 558.
4. Gilbert Haven and Thomas Russell, *Life of Father Taylor, the Sailor Preacher*, 266; Doug Adams, *Humor in the American Pulpit From George Whitefield Through Henry Ward Beecher*, 195.
5. Henry Ward Beecher, "The Ends and the Means," *Plymouth Pulpit*, III, 202; Doug Adams, *Humor in the American Pulpit*, 59.
6. Edward C. Hobbs, "The Gospel of Mark and the Exodus."
7. Elton Trueblood, *The Humor of Christ*, 63–64.
8. Robert M. Fowler, *Loaves and Fishes*, 117.
9. William Countryman, "How Many Basketsful," *Catholic Biblical Quarterly* 47 (1985): 643–55.
10. Robert Grant, "The Problem of Miraculous Feedings," *Protocol of the 42nd Colloquy*, 5.
11. Edward C. Hobbs, "Gospel Miracle Story and Modern Miracle Story," *Anglican Theological Review*, Supplemental Series, no. 3, 117–26.

Chapter 6. Love, Grandma:
The Fooling Humor of Paul's Letters

1. Phil Wiehe, "The Nose Knows," 6–7.
2. Doug Adams, "Paul as Humorist," 84–87; and "Paul as Grandmother," 10–11.
3. For discussion of digressions and other rhetorical strategies, see Wilhelm Wuellner's "Greek Rhetoric and Pauline Argumentation" in *Early Christian Literature and the Classical Intellectual Tradition*, 177–88.
4. Hans Dieter Betz, *Galatians: A Commentary on Paul's Letter to the Church in Galatia*, 270.

Chapter 7. Role Reversals in Dialogues Between the Finite and the Infinite: Bringing the Humor of Hebrew Scriptures to Life

1. See also Conrad Hyers, *The Comic Vision and the Christian Faith.*
2. E. B. White, "Some Remarks on Humor," in *The Second Tree from the Corner.*
3. I use the following pages of the Random House edition of Paddy Chayefsky's *Gideon* for a readers' theater presentation of twenty to thirty minutes: pages 5–11, 15 to the middle of 21, 24–30, 37 to the middle of 41, 45–47, 61, the bottom half of 84 to 85, 120 to the top of 134, 135 to the middle of 136, and 137–38.
4. The advice from three friends is a particularly satirical part of this play, as MacLeish has two of the three friends articulate modern schools of determinism instead of the fatalistic views of the Near Eastern world. For example, Bildad represents a Marxist view, while Eliphaz represents a Freudian view (pp. 119–23).
5. David Steele, *Slow Down, Moses,* 103. Some of his three dozen poems deal with New Testament humor; most deal with humor of Hebrew scriptures.
6. Norman J. Fedder, "Unstiffening Those Stiffnecked People," *Modern Liturgy* 12, no. 1 (1985): 12–14.

BIBLIOGRAPHY

Adams, Doug. "Bringing Biblical Humor to Life in Liturgy." *Modern Liturgy* 6, no. 8 (Dec. 1978/Jan. 1979): 4–5 and 27–29.

———. *Eyes to See Wholeness: Visual Arts Informing Biblical and Theological Studies in Education and Worship Through the Church Year.* Prescott, Ariz.: Educational Ministries, 1995.

———. *Humor in the American Pulpit from George Whitefield Through Henry Ward Beecher.* Austin, Tex.: The Sharing Co., 1975.

———. "Paul as Grandmother." *Modern Liturgy* 12, no. 1 (Feb. 1985): 10–11.

———. "Paul as Humorist." *The Bible Today* 33, no. 2 (Mar. 1995): 84–87.

———. "Wine and Humor at Cana." *The Fourth R* 5, no. 6 (Nov. 1992): 7–12.

Augustine. *The Confessions of Saint Augustine.* Ed. and trans. Edward B. Pussey. New York: Random House, 1949.

Bailey, Kenneth. *Poet and Peasant* and *Through Peasant Eyes.* Grand Rapids: William B. Eerdmans Publishing Co., 1983.

Beecher, Henry Ward. "Bearing One Another's Burdens." *The Sermons of Henry Ward Beecher in Plymouth Church, Brooklyn,* Eighth Series, 1872. New York: J. B. Ford & Co., 1873.

———. "The Ends and the Means." *Plymouth Pulpit,* III. Boston: Pilgrim Press, 1875.

Betz, Hans Dieter. *Galatians: A Commentary on Paul's Letter to the Church in Galatia.* Philadelphia: Fortress Press, 1979.

Breech, James. *Jesus and Postmodernism.* Minneapolis: Fortress Press, 1989.

————. *The Silence of Jesus: The Authentic Voice of the Historical Man.* Philadelphia: Fortress Press, 1983.

Browne, E. Martin, ed. *Religious Drama 2: Mystery and Miracle Plays.* New York: World Publishing Group, 1958.

Calvin, John. *Institutes of the Christian Religion,* vol. 2. Trans. Henry Beveridge. Grand Rapids: William B. Eerdmans Publishing Co., 1970.

Chayefsky, Paddy. *Gideon.* New York: Random House, 1965.

Countryman, William. "How Many Basketsful: Mark 8:14–21 and the Values of Miracles in Mark." *Catholic Biblical Quarterly* 47 (Oct. 1985): 643–55.

Crossan, John Dominic. *The Dark Interval: Towards a Theology of Story.* Valencia, Calif.: Argus Communications, 1975; Sonoma, Calif.: Polebridge Press, 1988.

————. *Raid on the Articulate: Comic Eschatology in Jesus and Borges.* New York: Harper & Row, 1976.

Donne, John. *The Sermons of John Donne,* vol. 2. Ed. George Potter and Evelyn M. Simpson. Berkeley, Calif.: University of California Press, 1955.

Fedder, Norman J. "Unstiffening Those Stiffnecked People: 5 Improvisations," *Modern Liturgy* 12, no. 1 (Feb. 1985): 12–14.

Fowler, Robert. *Loaves and Fishes: The Function of the Feeding Stories in the Gospel of Mark.* Chico, Calif.: Scholars Press, 1981.

Funk, Robert W. *Jesus as Precursor.* Philadelphia: Fortress Press, 1975; Sonoma, Calif.: Polebridge Press, 1994.

Grant, Robert. "The Problem of Miraculous Feedings in the Graeco-Roman Period." In *Protocol of the 42nd Colloquy.* Berkeley, Calif.: Center for Hermeneutical Studies, 1982.

Groves, Jim, and Terry Teigen. "Dramatizing Humor in Jonah, Chapter 4." *Modern Liturgy* 6, no. 8 (Dec. 1978/Jan. 1979): 8.

Haven, Gilbert, and Thomas Russell. *Life of Father Taylor, the Sailor Preacher.* Boston: Boston Port and Seaman's Aid Society, 1904.

Herzog, William. *Parables as Subversive Speech: Jesus as Pedagogue of the Oppressed.* Louisville, Ky.: Westminster John Knox Press, 1994.

Hobbs, Edward C. "Gospel Miracle Story and Modern Miracle Story."

Anglican Theological Review, Supplemental Series, no. 3 (Mar. 1974), 117–26.

———. "The Gospel of Mark and the Exodus." University of Chicago, Ph.D. diss., 1958.

Hyers, Conrad. *And God Created Laughter: The Bible as Divine Comedy.* Atlanta: John Knox Press, 1987.

———. *The Comic Vision and the Christian Faith: A Celebration of Life and Laughter.* New York: Pilgrim Press, 1981.

———. *Meaning of Creation: Genesis and Modern Science.* Atlanta: John Knox Press, 1984.

Kierkegaard, Søren. *The Concept of Irony.* Trans. Lee M. Capel. Bloomington, Ind.: Indiana University Press, 1971.

Kiffmeyer, John. "Translating Scripture to Hear Humor." *Modern Liturgy* 6, no. 8 (Dec. 1978/Jan. 1979): 6–7.

Luccock, Halford. "Research: Human Interest and Humorous Stories of the Church." *Christian Century* (July 7, 1954): 817.

MacLeish, Archibald. *J.B.* Cambridge: Riverside Press, 1956.

Moynahan, Michael. *Once Upon a Miracle: Dramas for Worship and Religious Education.* New York: Paulist Press, 1993.

———. *Once Upon a Parable: Dramas for Worship and Religious Education.* New York: Paulist Press, 1984.

Odets, Clifford. *The Flowering Peach.* New York: Dramatists Play Service, n.d.

Radday, Yehuda, and Athalya Brenner. *On Humor and the Comic in the Hebrew Bible.* Sheffield: Sheffield Academic Press, 1990.

Sanders, James A. *God Has a Story Too: Sermons in Context.* Philadelphia: Fortress Press, 1979.

———. "The Ethic of Election in Luke's Great Banquet Parable," in *Luke and Scripture: The Function of Sacred Tradition in Luke-Acts.* Ed. Craig A. Evans and James A. Sanders. Minneapolis: Fortress Press, 1993.

Steele, David. *Slow Down, Moses: A Light-Hearted Look at People in the Bible.* Minneapolis: Augsburg, 1990.

Taylor, Gardner C. *How Shall They Preach?* Elgin, Ill.: Progressive Baptist Publishing House, 1977.

———. *The Scarlet Thread: Nineteen Sermons.* Elgin, Ill.: Progressive Baptist Publishing House, 1981.

Tipple, Ezra Squier. *Drew Theological Seminary, 1867–1917: A Review of the First Half Century*. New York: Methodist Book Concern, 1917.

Trueblood, Elton. *The Humor of Christ*. New York: Harper & Row, 1964.

White, E. B. "Some Remarks on Humor." *The Second Tree from the Corner*. New York: Harper & Brothers, 1954.

Wiehe, Phil. "The Nose Knows." *Modern Liturgy* 9, no. 2 (Mar./Apr. 1982): 6–7.

Wuellner, Wilhelm. "Greek Rhetoric and Pauline Argumentation." In *Early Christian Literature and the Classical Intellectual Tradition*. Ed. William R. Schoedel and Robert L. Wilken, 177–88. Paris: Editing Beauchesne, 1980.

INDEX